Ken Wytsma writes like an old master. His books contain the echoes of Oxford pubs, the sea-sprays of cliffside churches, and the woodsmoke of myth tellers. *Create vs. Copy* is Ken at his very best.

— **Dr. John Sowers,** president and CEO of The Mentoring Project

If you want to find your life, lose it. If you want to be great, become the least. . . . At the heart of the Christian faith there is a grand paradox, but it requires *imagination* if we are to have eyes to see and ears to hear. Ken Wytsma refuses to see the world in black and white. *Create vs. Copy* is an invitation to live in full color.

— **Shane Claiborne,** author, activist, recovering sinner
www.redletterchristians.org

In *Create vs. Copy* Ken brings his unique integrationist approach straight to the heart of leadership and influence in a way that is sure to reform leader toolkits across many platforms and excite a generation of would-be leaders to lean heavy into their imaginations and creativity as they breathe life into the world.

— **Leroy Barber,** cofounder of The VOICES Project and author of
Everyday Missions

Create vs. Copy masterfully articulates the nuanced realities of creativity through the lens of theology and practice. Ken rightly compels us to embrace the redemptive purpose and power of creativity in a world that desperately longs for its presence.

— **Charles Lee,** CEO of Ideation and author of *Good Idea. Now What?*

Theologically grounded and practical in application, *Create vs. Copy* will inspire you to explore your God-given gift of creativity. Drawing on his experience as a social entrepreneur, church planter, and justice advocate, Ken is the right person to help each of us uncork our creative spirit.

— **Peter Greer,** president and CEO, HOPE International and coauthor
of *Mission Drift*

Ken is one of the most creative guys I know, and he's written another terrific book—this time about the power of our imaginations to shape our lives, our world, and our faith.

— **Bob Goff,** author, *Love Does*, founder, Restore International

Do you want to be a creator? If so, Ken Wytsma is the guide you need to the true heart of leadership and influence. *Create vs. Copy* is the gold standard for inspiring leaders to make their mark.

— **Claire Diaz-Ortiz,** author, speaker, Silicon Valley innovator

Create vs. Copy will electrify our imaginations, as it challenges us to new, redemptive ways of seeing and steers us toward the flourishing that God intends for the world.

— **C. Christopher Smith,** coauthor of *Slow Church* and founding editor
of *The Englewood Review of Books*

Ken invites us to imagine new possibilities and new futures as we embrace our role as co-creators with God. In my context here in Asia, where "copying" is almost an art form, Ken's fresh call to innovation and imagination is a word in season for both the church and the marketplace.

— **Andrew Gardener,** lead pastor of The Vine Center in Hong Kong
and cofounder of The Justice Conference Asia

Creativity is much lauded today, but too often is mistaken for mimicry. In this punchy and powerful book, Ken Wytsma steers us away from the contemporary cult of constant copying and plugs us into the source of all originality—the Creator himself. *Create vs. Copy* is an essential resource for anyone engaged in partnering with God as He re-creates the world.

— **Mark Sayers,** pastor of Red Church in Melbourne, Australia, and author of
Facing Leviathan

In *Create vs. Copy*, Ken Wytsma has accomplished something significant. He provides principles for thinking theologically about creativity and practical insights for leveraging imagination and innovation in all of life. This book will help you think and dream in whole new ways. I highly recommend it.

— **Stephan Bauman,** president and CEO, World Relief, author,
Possible: A Blueprint for Changing How We Change the World.

To call *Create vs. Copy* a "how-to" book would be erroneous but rather, this is a much needed book that will inspire imagination and creativity that will ultimately impact our spirituality, leadership, and daily living.

— **Eugene Cho,** founder, One Day's Wages, Author, *Overrated: Are We More in
Love With the Idea of Changing the World Than Actually Changing the World?*

Creating is one of the most healing things we can do for ourselves and for this world. Yet it is inherently difficult. Ken walks with us in this tension, helping us recognize our own creative spirit and honor the creative spirit of others, so we can better lead, love, parent, play, and exercise the Spirit of God in us. We need this book.

— **Allison Vesterfelt,** author, *Packing Light: Thoughts on Living Life with Less
Baggage*

create

EMBRACE CHANGE.
IGNITE CREATIVITY.
BREAK THROUGH
WITH IMAGINATION.

vs. copy

ken wytsma

MOODY PUBLISHERS
CHICAGO

All Scripture quotations are taken from the Holy Bible, New International Version®, NIV®. Copyright © 1973, 1978, 1984, 2011 by Biblica, Inc.™ Used by permission of Zondervan. All rights reserved worldwide. www.zondervan.com. The "NIV" and "New International Version" are trademarks registered in the United States Patent and Trademark Office by Biblica, Inc.™

All italics or bolded text shown in Scripture quotations have been added by the author.

Edited by Matthew Boffey
Interior Design: Erik Peterson
Interior Illustrations: Paul Crouse
Cover Design: Faceout Studio, Jeff Miller
Author Photo: Benjamin Edwards Photography

Library of Congress Cataloging-in-Publication Data

Names: Wytsma, Ken, author.
Title: Create vs. copy : embrace change, ignite creativity, break through
  with imagination / Ken Wytsma.
Description: Chicago : Moody Publishers, [2015]
Identifiers: LCCN 2015037981 | ISBN 9780802413499
Subjects: LCSH: Creative ability—Religious aspects—Christianity. | Change
  (Psychology)—Religious aspects—Christianity.
Classification: LCC BT709.5 .W97 2015 | DDC 153.3/5—dc23 LC record available at
http://lccn.loc.gov/2015037981

All websites and phone numbers listed herein are accurate at the time of publication but may change in the future or cease to exist. The listing of website references and resources does not imply publisher endorsement of the site's entire contents. Groups and organizations are listed for informational purposes, and listing does not imply publisher endorsement of their activities.

We hope you enjoy this book from Moody Publishers. Our goal is to provide high-quality, thought-provoking books and products that connect truth to your real needs and challenges. For more information on other books and products written and produced from a biblical perspective, go to www.moodypublishers.com or write to:

Moody Publishers
820 N. LaSalle Boulevard
Chicago, IL 60610

1 3 5 7 9 10 8 6 4 2

Printed in the United States of America

To my father, Johannes Wytsma,
for stirring in me a love of wisdom.

Also by Ken Wytsma

Pursuing Justice:
The Call to Live and Die for Bigger Things

The Grand Paradox:
The Messiness of Life, the Mystery of God,
and the Necessity of Faith

Contents

*Creativity means
not copying.*

Ferran Adrià, *Washington Post*, Oct. 11, 2011

WARHOL
VAN GOGH,
MICHELANGELO
PICASSO, DA VINCI,
REMBRANDT, DEGAS, MONET,
GOYA, LICHTENSTEIN, TURNER,
RAPHAEL, O'KEEFFE, SCHIELE,

Introduction

It is better to fail in originality than to succeed in imitation.

Herman Melville

In the last decade, I've come to believe that the ability leaders need more than any other is the ability to innovate and encourage innovation in others.

In my 20s I read a lot of leadership books. Leadership books can be both inspiring and helpful. As I've moved into my 40s, however, I've found that as an entrepreneur (and even as a parent) I have a growing desire to understand and harness the role of creativity in life—to innovate.

When I and my wife, Tamara, started a church in 2006, I thought we would have all the vision and strategy mapped out for our new community. As it turned out, we came into the launch season after some difficult and disappointing times. Instead of applying all the leadership principles I had gleaned over the years, it felt like we were walking into the future facing backwards. In place of tidy vision documents, we leaned on faith.

I don't know if this is entirely the best way to enter into a church startup, but it taught us a lot about reading the gifts of the people in front of us and discerning the opportunities each moment or season offered. We learned the value of collaboration and creativity in forming spiritual community. We had to; we couldn't do what we'd always done. We had to innovate.

The truth is, whether a CEO, nonprofit worker, or parent, how we respond to the challenges of modern culture will define our success, our happiness, and our legacy. It is as important as ever to understand how God has made us creative and how creativity works.

But are we equipped for this?

Far too often leadership has been spoken of in either cold terms: management principles for effectiveness and efficiency, or elite terms: only certain people—with the right pedigree, platform, or personality—are true leaders.

Leadership, however, is undergoing a revolution.

It is moving from static to more dynamic forms. Additionally, with the advent of social media and globalization, men and women from all walks of life are exerting a much greater degree of influence and leadership than possibly ever before. Think about it, how many people can you influence at this moment if you accessed all the communication channels at your disposal? Leadership is becoming broadly a human trait.

In answer to the age-old question, "Are leaders born or made?" the answer is *both*. We are all born into interconnected roles of influence and can grow in our ability to leverage gifting, calling, and responsibility in affecting the people and culture around us.

If leadership is traditionally spoken of in cold or elite terms, creativity is traditionally spoken of in whimsical terms: what children or dreamers get to focus on, or exclusive terms: that creativity is the realm of the artists among us—those who paint, write poetry, and have a knack for self-expression.

I believe that creativity, like leadership and influence, is for all of us.

The rate of change in society today leaves many people afraid. Afraid they can't keep up. Afraid they won't like the world of tomorrow. Afraid in general.

God didn't create us to live in fear. Rather, God made us

creative so we could navigate threats and challenges, laying hold of the possibilities around us.

Creativity elevates us. It's standing on our tiptoes and looking over the backyard fence. It is often all the difference we need to navigate the current of our circumstances.

Two Kinds of People

I believe there are two kinds of people in the world: those who *create* and those who *copy*.

Those who create blaze trails, take risks, and try new ways.

They ask, "Why not?" They innovate. They respond to challenges, not with fear, but with imagination.

They lead.

Creators certainly borrow ideas and use what already exists as building blocks, but their mindset is one of possibility and exploration, not duplication.

Copying certainly yields results, but to blaze a trail we must create. Copiers, by definition, will always *follow*.

Copying is also a mindset. It is one that believes the *only* way forward is to find someone to emulate. To *only* seek proven strategies or doors that have been opened.

It collapses possibility. It doesn't dream.

It doesn't lean into imagination or creativity. It defaults to pragmatism.

The distinction between those who would create and those who would copy is no small thing. In fact, it is the backbone of this book. I truly believe there is a wealth of untapped creative energy available to people if we could break the chains of the copier mentality, find courage in our creative identities, and unleash the power of imagination.

Think about it: every apocalyptic movie that wants to show the human race as enslaved paints them as robotically following and copying. They don't think for themselves. They don't dream or imagine. They are lifeless masses trapped in a posture of automatic mindless behavior. The hero in these futuristic movies is the one who breaks the mold and awakens people once more to their humanity—their *creativity*!

Some, of course, will push back and say that creativity can't be separated from copying. And, in many ways, it can't.

A distinction is needed, and we'll explore that more in a bit.

For now, let's acknowledge the wisdom of the speaker in Ecclesiastes: "There is nothing new under the sun." The building blocks are all around us, and much of creativity is a rearranging of component parts.

That's essentially what this book is about: using the creativity within us to engage with what's around us. It is about exploring our God-given creativity and how it can direct our influence.

In part 1, we'll explore the theology behind creativity. We'll look at how God created us to be creative, how that creativity is ongoing, and how that creativity is redemptive. We'll also briefly explore the nature of globalization and hear from some voices on the front lines of global change and innovation.

In part 2, we'll explore the practice of bringing about more creativity in our lives. We'll examine how we often neglect imagination as we age and look at practical ways to fan the flames of creativity in our lives.

Creators have a mindset of
**POSSIBILITY &
EXPLORATION,**
not duplication.

The future of influence requires *intentional* creativity, and the opportunities of today require, more than ever, the ability to imagine what *can* be. They require constant creativity. They require innovation.

Innovation simply is the application of new ideas or methods to an established way of doing something. It's the result of purposeful application of creativity to our challenges, opportunities, and systems.

Innovation reanimates dead communities, movements, and institutions. It transforms threats into opportunities. It breathes peace into panic and hope into despair.

Today's influencers simply can't succeed without appreciating the role of creativity.

But this is where it gets really exciting.

We have the ability to shape culture instead of merely reacting to it.

Yes, I am interested in the effectiveness and efficiency that comes from modern leadership and sound business principles. But I am *passionate* about the success that comes from submitting these ideas to God's direction, refining them with a theology of creativity, and infusing them with imagination. That's what this book is about.

A theology of creativity sees innovation as more than a smart business tactic. It is an integral part of our relationship with creation and our role in reality. As we'll see in the first chapter, human beings are born to create. If we are born to create, innovation isn't just about harnessing creativity—it's actually about restoring creativity to its rightful place at the heart of all we do.

This book is about creativity.

It is about possibility.

It is about unleashing your imagination.

It is not a book aimed at artists.

It is not a how-to for copiers.

Rather, this book is meant to encourage you about the good news of your God-given creative capacity and how to harness it to take charge of your life, flourish, succeed, and find innovative and exciting ways to navigate the circumstances of life.

— **Ken Wytsma**

#CreatevsCopy

Part 1

*There are painters who
transform the sun to a yellow
spot, but there are others who,
with the help of their art and
their intelligence, transform
a yellow spot into a sun.*
Picasso

nking
about
ativity

Chapter 1

To Create Is Divine

Fantasy remains a human right: we make in our measure and in our derivative mode, because we are made: and not only made, but made in the image and likeness of a Maker.

J. R. R. Tolkien, "On Fairy Stories"

How would you depict God in a work of art?

That's the provocative question I found myself asking on a recent trip to Rome. Standing with my daughter underneath Michelangelo's world-famous work in the Sistine Chapel, we couldn't help but be taken in by the most recognized image in the entire building: *The Creation of Adam*. Situated near the center of the ceiling, the fresco shows God reaching His finger toward Adam to create humanity.

In the painting—probably the most iconic depiction of God in the world—God is a powerfully built, elderly European man with sinewy arms, long gray hair, and a beard. Adam is naked, reclining, and seems to be only halfheartedly reaching back to God. Michelangelo had wrapped his Greek ideas about physical beauty, symmetry, and the body into his portrayal of the image of God, as well as his ideas about humanity's relationship to God.

Was he right?

Created to Create

There's an element of the image of God we almost never talk about. It's strange we leave it out, because it's the very first thing we learn about God. In grad school theology courses I explored God's attributes, what He is like—He is rational, holy, relational, and so on. But almost never did my studies hit this fundamental property of God: He is *creative*.

Genesis 1:27 says, "So God created mankind in his own image, in the image of God he created them; male and female he created them."

Looking solely at the words in this sentence, what is the one thing we read about the nature of God?

Simple. God *creates*.

The only thing we can know with grammatical certainty about the image of God from this verse, then, is that it necessarily involves creativity.

God is immensely creative. We all know that too many colors in a painting or living room can be dissonant, but when I walk in the mountains, forests, and deserts of Central Oregon, where I live, I am astounded at how God is able to bring hundreds of colors into beautiful, consonant harmony. From the alpine lakes to the patches of colored wildflowers in spring, nothing in the landscape ever seems to clash or fail in the beauty of God's nature. Have you ever marveled at how God has made thousands of colors sing together without clashing? It's hard for us to add three or four colors to an outfit before it starts to clash, let alone the myriad hues we see in mountain meadows.

The same impression hits me when I look to the sky. Incredible sunsets are delightful, and their timing always seems perfect. They are alive in the moment and deeply inspiring. It shows the touch of the Master Artist, who paints in real time.

The late Francis Schaeffer saw this property of God in a rather obscure place. In his book *Art and the Bible* he talks about the specifications that God gave for priestly garments: "Make pomegranates of blue, purple and scarlet yarn around the hem of the robe" (Exod. 28:33). Schaeffer used this verse to make the argument that God, who could have told them to make the pomegranates red (the color of dye their skins were

> # When we study creativity or act creatively,
> # **WE LEARN ABOUT GOD.**

used for in the ancient world), ordered that they be a blend of yarn that would give a lifelike and representative feel. Put another way, it was a form of impressionistic art. God doesn't color like a child. His creativity manifests beautifully in everything He does.

When we study creativity or act creatively, we learn about God.

As those made in God's image, we bear the hints of His creativity within us. Put another way, we will never exemplify God's image in us to the fullest without exercising creativity. I like to say that when we're being creative, it's as if we're taking the image of God in us out for a walk. Creativity is one way we manifest and exercise the image of God.

When we hold a child in our arms, pursue justice for our oppressed neighbor, or cry out in prayer and worship, we know that we are relating to our Creator in a profound way. Similarly, creativity can connect us with our Creator, opening the future in surprising ways.

But more than just having the capacity to be creative, we also have a *responsibility* to be creative. One of the first things God asked Adam to do—shortly before the creation of Eve—was to tend and care for a garden (Genesis 2:15). Later, God asked Adam to name the animals (2:19–20). God was certainly capable of both tasks, but He seems to be encouraging and nurturing human creativity even in the midst of creating the foundations of the world.

When people say, "I don't have a creative bone in my body," not only is it untrue, it's denying the image of God in us. While artistic ability is a talent a select few possess (and/or cultivate with time and hard work), creative capacity is something *all of us* are born with. Put another way, artists are skilled with unique talents, but creativity is part of what makes us human. Madeleine L'Engle, the famed author of *A Wrinkle in Time* and many other novels, says it well:

> *But unless we are creators we are not fully alive.*
> *What do I mean by creators? Not only artists, whose*
> *acts of creation are the obvious ones of working with*
> *paint or clay or words. Creativity is a way of living*
> *life, no matter our vocation or how we earn our*
> *living. Creativity is not limited to the arts, or having*
> *some kind of important career.*[1]

So while we're not all Michelangelo, we're all creators nonetheless. Fulfilling our mandate to create can take many different forms.

Let me illustrate with a story from the church where I pastor, Antioch. As a church we've always celebrated creativity—its integral role in our souls as beings made in God's image, the ability for *everyone* to share in the creative process, etc.—and we wanted to help the community celebrate it, too. So we invited people to showcase their creativity on Art Sunday. From cooking to floral arrangements to photography to poetry to woodworking, we were blown away—not only by how much amazing art came forward, but how creative *everyone* seemed to be. Teachers, mortgage brokers, bankers, computer technicians—the list goes on—all contributed something to Art Sunday.

It changed my conception of art. The amazingly wide base of creativity displayed that day broadened my narrow conception of what it means to be creative.

Art is to creativity as science is to knowledge. We might not all be scientists, but we all live within the realm of rationality and knowledge. Likewise, we might not all be artists, but we all live in a creatively charged world. I might not paint with a brush, but I make plans on the weekend, make my own variation on recipes, and name my own pets. I may not sell my creations, but I do live them.

Too often we tell ourselves that only artists are creative, but creativity is a gift we have all been given. *Everyone* made in the image of God participates in this reality. Despite the wide belief that some people have more creative genes than others, psychologist Robert Epstein, PhD, a visiting scholar at the University of California, states, "There's not really any evidence one person is *inherently* more creative than another" (emphasis mine).[2] Artistic ability is a talent some possess, but creativity is a human trait.

Think about what you create:

> Ideas
> Products
> Memories
> Recipes
> Sculptures
> Football plays in a pickup game
> Organizations
> Floral arrangements
> Prayer groups
> Vacation plans
> Kickstarter campaigns
> Bucket lists
> Ways to encourage others
> Adventures
> Friendships

Community
Online posts
Jokes
Ways to show love
Ways to organize
And ways of doing thousands of other things.

Much of what you do in life, you create. You probably don't need convincing of that. But here's what I want to suggest: Though we often use creativity, we only partially understand it, and we rarely *intentionalize* it.

What do I mean by *intentionalize*? I mean making the effort to take our creativity for a walk—and on uncharted routes. God expects us to be creative, just as He expects us to be loving and patient, and so on.

If we don't intentionally use and develop our creativity, there will be certain problems we can never solve. Certain projects

ARTISTIC ABILITY
is a talent some possess.

CREATIVITY
is a human trait.

we can never undertake. Certain relationships we will never enjoy. Creativity opens up new horizons in our relationship with God, with our families and communities, and even with the world.

Creativity is a game changer.

Creators vs. Copiers

Some proudly use the word "copy" as a kind of bravado of honesty and transparency. In this vein, Picasso is attributed with saying, "Good artists copy, great artists steal," and Einstein with, "The secret to creativity is knowing how to hide your sources." Or as Voltaire more mildly put it, "Originality is nothing but judicious imitation. The most original writers borrowed one from another."[3]

I think we all understand and can appreciate this sense of the word *copy*. After all, only God creates *completely* from scratch.[4] The adage for us is this: If it works, borrow it. If it doesn't, ignore it.

It's an honest admission that we all have been shaped by a thousand hands, and much of our creative energy takes inspiration from what we have seen, experienced, and appreciated. I recently heard Cornel West say it like this: "Nobody steps into the Hall of Fame alone."[5]

The sense of *copy* I'm using is neither the playful one nor the authentic one just described.

Rather, I'm talking about "copying" as a mindset that refuses to consider new ideas and new relationships. This kind of copying is a habit of never thinking outside the box, never adapting to rapid change, never being willing to fail. This kind of copying simply takes what is known and safe and repeats it *ad infinitum*.

Creators, on the other hand, do borrow much . . . but for the purpose of making things new. The Renaissance artists of Florence borrowed from Greek myths, humanism, and Roman architecture, but always with the mindset of *transforming*— not merely copying—what had come before.

That's God's call to us as well: don't just be copiers, but creators. We've all been given things from which to borrow: family histories, jobs, talents and skills, interests and hobbies—even our race and gender, the country we live in, our language, schooling, and stage of life. Out of this raw material God invites us to create, to move forward into the fullest expression of God's creative image in us. We are being asked to reject copying in order to create, extend, and breathe life into what is meant to flourish.

So we find things that work. We study our heroes and learn about best practices. But we maintain a mindset of creativity and always look to transform rather than merely replicate.

We Breathe Life

Creativity is about responding to God's image and call—and *through that response, exerting a creative influence and leadership the world is desperate to follow.*

Genesis 1:2 says, "Now the earth was formless and empty, darkness was over the surface of the deep." God chose to create within that environment, so we shouldn't be surprised when we find ourselves in the midst of formless, void things. And we shouldn't be unsure about what we need to do.

Have you ever counseled a friend? Taught a child to search for animals in the clouds above? Cultivated a garden? Named a dog?

All of those things are creative acts, reflecting the creative image of our Creator.

We breathe life into our families when we come up with creative ways of making memories. We breathe life into our industry when we come up with a different way of doing business. We breathe life into our churches when we discover new ways of expressing our two-thousand-year-old beliefs and doctrines.

Creativity is meant to be life-giving, because it is part of God's image in us.

For further study at KenWytsma.com

1. A List of Quotes on Art, Beauty, and Creativity
2. 4 Books Everyone Should Read on Creativity and Why
3. Interview with Charles Lee on *Good Idea. Now What?*

Questions for Group, Team, or Individual Reflection

1. Have you been affirmed in your creativity, or have you been stifled? How?
2. If you were to participate in an Art Sunday, what could you contribute? Think beyond just your first idea or two.
3. What are the raw materials in your life that you have to work with?

#CreatevsCopy

Chapter 2

Continuous Creativity

*We are ourselves creations. We are meant to
continue creativity by being creative ourselves . . .
Creativity is God's gift to us. Using creativity is our
gift back to God.*

Julia Cameron, *Heart Steps*

One of the few things I remember from my mechanical engi-
neering class in college is the Second Law of Thermodynamics.
Ironically, it's burned into my mind because of how badly I
failed a test on it! The famous second law is credited primarily
to the French physicist Said Carnot, but the four laws of thermodynamics were the result of extensive studies by scientists
throughout the mid-1800s. The second law remains one of the
most famous and quoted laws of the four, and physicists hold it
as a rock-solid axiom. It goes something like this:

*All closed systems tend to move toward a state of greater disorder
and dissipated energy.*

Also known as the Law of Increased Entropy, this law states that in a closed system (where no new energy can enter) all activity will eventually decay as entropy increases. This is why heat naturally flows from hotter to colder objects until the whole system reaches equilibrium, or why stars burn out, fires turn to ashes, and machines wear down.

Closed systems are doomed to dissipate.

Our Systems Can Be Open

This dissipation is familiar in nearly every area of life. If not renewed, donor bases will erode over time. Congregations will shrink. Family dynamics will tense up. Relationships will fade. Leadership strategies become stale and ineffective. Even our bodies and minds lose their vigor.

Though this could be a discouraging idea to some, it actually brings me comfort: I'm not the only one who feels helpless in the face of relentless, merciless entropy. Change and deterioration of the *status quo* are not signals that the world is ending; rather, they're a natural part of the world we live in.

Things decay.

Here's what's so vital to our understanding of creative leadership: This decay and eventual "death" is irreversible, *but only in a closed system.*

The law of entropy only holds when there are no external inputs of energy into the system. In a system that isn't fixed or closed, however, the game is wide open.

Creativity is our way to crack the system open.

If systems are decaying but open, then creative change can mean renewal. In fact, the word "innovation" derives from the fifteenth-century Latin word *innovationem*: "restoration or renewal."[1] Restoration and renewal are ways of fighting entropy, injecting life into dying systems.

Unfortunately, many of us think that such creativity and innovation isn't our domain. In the same way that culture tells us creativity is for "artists," it tells us that innovation is only for entrepreneurs. We think innovators are an elite class of people like Thomas Edison or Elon Musk.

However, creativity and innovation are things we are naturally capable of as humans. Planting a rooftop garden in a troubled inner city is an act of renewal. Developing a new way to communicate more effectively and positively with your teenager is an act of restoration.

As Christians, we cannot allow society's assumptions to disempower the imaginative and creative potential around us and *within* us. It is part of God's image in us, and it is meant to be an ongoing part of how we respond to God.

In 2012, Nicole Baker Fulgham founded the Expectations Project, an organization empowering people of faith to shine a light on education inequality through prayer, service, and advocacy. As an educator, Fulgham saw an education system that many define as "broken" and imagined what it could be, what it could accomplish if only a handful of churches and Christians around the country reimagined their relationship with it—with the administrators, the faculty, and most importantly the students.

"I've seen the church be such a force with other societal challenges, and I believe we can have the same impact on our education system and schools," says Fulgham.[2]

The Expectations Project looked at data that had been available for years, most of which pointed toward a bleak future for a number of school districts around the country. But where others saw hopelessness, Fulgham saw opportunity.

There are more than 300,000 places of worship across America, compared with roughly 50,000 high-poverty public schools struggling to meet students' needs.

That's a 6 to 1 ratio.

That's a creative solution to a gigantic problem.

What if those 300,000 churches were informed, equipped, and empowered to engage in the public school system in a way that's never been done before?

Rather than letting the academic achievement gap continue to widen and the school system to decay, Fulgham imagined a way to crack the system open, to breathe new life and energy into it. And guess what? It's working.

"We've seen congregations in Indiana stand up to demand preschool options for low-income families," says Fulgham. "Churches in Washington, DC, have requested the expansion of high-quality school options for kids in the most challenged neighborhoods. And churches all around the nation are finding creative, impactful ways to partner with schools and families to improve student outcomes."

As leaders identify culture, systems, or strategies that are tending toward disorder or death, they are uniquely positioned to harness the image of God in us and breathe in new life. Much like God's initial creative act, a timely innovation or burst of creativity can break the cycle of death and decay or breathe life into a space where before there was nothing.

Yes, the world is changing—and often decaying—but to creatures made in the image of an immeasurably creative God, *the system is open*. **In fact, it is God who leads us in the way of continuous creativity.**

God Is Still Creating

In the first part of what I call a "Theology of Creativity," we saw the fundamental truth that we are inherently creators made in the image of a creative God.

A second facet of the creativity of God, or tenet of a theology of creativity, can be seen in Isaiah 54:15–17:

> *If anyone does attack you, it will not be my doing;*
> *whoever attacks you will surrender to you.*
> *"See, **it is I who created the blacksmith***
> ***who fans the coals into flame***
> ***and forges a weapon fit for its work.***
> *And it is I who have created the destroyer to wreak*
> *havoc; no weapon forged against you will prevail,*
> *and you will refute every tongue that accuses you.*
> *This is the heritage of the servants of the Lord,*
> *and this is their vindication from me,"*
> *declares the Lord.*

We are all familiar with the idea of God as Creator—that He created the heavens and the earth—but the passage above was meant to communicate to God's people that He *also* created the blacksmith and is over the weapons of war that held people captive to fear. In other words, God was still creating in the Israelites' context, and he had control over the people and circumstances they feared. This is still the case today. This is what is captured in the biblical idea of God as the potter with His hands *actively* molding our lives as clay.

Our Creator God is still actively involved in His creation, which can bring relief as we look to Him for aid and comfort. When Jesus calmed the storm, His disciples were comforted (even if also shocked) by His control over creation—it was God's active power and strength they were experiencing.

God has created and continues to create, but there is one more dimension to this: He will *keep* creating.

In Isaiah 65:17–18, God seeks to comfort His people by declaring, "See, **I will create** new heavens and a new earth. The former things will not be remembered, nor will they come to mind. But be glad and rejoice forever in what **I will create**, for **I will create** Jerusalem to be a delight and its people a joy."

God's promise that He would create goodness into the future was the source of joy for His people. God's creativity through time and into the future brings hope. We live in confidence that, no matter how tense the story, the end is not yet written; it is fully under the control of the Storyteller—our creative God.

Put another way, God *created (in the past), is creating (now), and will create (in the future).* Creativity isn't something that only happens at one point in time. Rather, with God, it is a continuous process of creation, a natural outflowing of the character of God. It doesn't end, and it isn't supposed to.

We Are Still Creating, Too

In chapter 1, I made the case that creativity is part of the image of God in *all* of us. If our creativity is a reflection of the divine spark with which He has imbued humanity, is there also an eternal or ongoing potential to our creative nature?

There is.

We, like God, have created in the past, are creating now, and can create into the future.

One of the mistakes we make with creativity is to study it as if under a microscope, which is a natural tendency when we study things. But slides under a microscope are frozen. They're not dynamic, and they don't extend through time. Slides and microscopes point to closed systems.

To fully understand something, it also has to be seen in context and in extension through time—and even into eternity.

Christians who study salvation under a microscope tend to reduce it to a single moment of forgiveness, which highlights the transaction of salvation but removes the process.

One of the hallmarks of the Christian tradition of salvation, however, is the idea that it's a process: I *have been* saved, *am being* saved, and someday *will be* saved when I arrive at heaven's gates. (Theologians have words for these three parts of salvation: *justification, sanctification,* and *glorification.*)

Similarly, a full understanding of a theology of creativity should allow us to see God's creative act through time. The one who made us and continues to move in and about us will also someday fulfill His creative aims by establishing our joy in the new heavens and new earth.

The correlation through time of God's saving work and His creative energy can be expressed visually like so:

We tend to think deep and long about theology when it comes to salvation. Why not think just as long and deep about a theology of creativity and the nature of God's work through time?

Not only is God still actively participating in creation, but He also says He *will* create. God's promises and His creative energy extend into the future. The God who knit you together in your mother's womb is still actively involved in your world, continues to create, and will continue His creation into eternity where it will be perfected.

The comforting bottom line is this: we are not left alone to try to find our way out of the mess through our own labor and creativity. We can find hope and confidence that God is present in our struggle to overcome the things in front of us. Just as God has saved us, is saving us, and will ultimately perfect our salvation, He has created the world, is still actively creating it through and with us, and will ultimately perfect His creation in eternity.

Your world is *not* a closed-system.

Creativity is a way we can speak to the present and engage the future.

Creativity as Response

Harnessing continuous creativity or creative potential is a fitting, wise, and hope-filled response to the circumstances that challenge us.

Consider globalization. Deep inside, we all feel the effects of a fast-paced, worldwide culture filled with constant change. We are flooded with information, sometimes over-connected socially, and exposed to realities in the world that boggle our minds and dizzy us. When we think about "the world," we can feel overwhelmed or helpless. The temptation, then, is to focus on ourselves. Sticking to what we know is one way to avoid dealing with what we don't know.

But God is sovereign even over global change. The Bible says He raises up kings and nations and also brings them down. God creates and moves through time. He is over history.

God might today remind us He created the banker who owns our loan. That He is over our debt and our stress. That He created the entrepreneurs driving much of the change in the world. Or that He created the people standing in opposition to you at work. That He is over your church, which is struggling to move beyond its out-of-date habits and engage the world creatively.

This continuous creativity happens in our families as well. It can be scary for a family with teenagers to realize they need to reshape family culture to the new demands of adolescence and all it brings. It's scary for someone living month-to-month financially to think outside the box or feel free to do anything other than react to the threat of financial crisis.

Embracing creativity can be scary, especially when internally you don't feel creative. It takes energy and courage to allow yourself to dream or create when your natural insecurities have always been fed with voices telling you you're not innovative or creative.

Remember, however, that embracing creativity is embracing what's already inside of you. It's about being fully human. It's a recognition that the challenges in front of you don't define your existence and aren't the totality of the world. Instead, the challenges are located in a dynamic environment over which God sits sovereign and within which God has placed a creative, problem-solving being: you.

Every day, in simple, relatable ways, you can start responding to the world, as God does, with continuous creativity.

Here are five ways to be more creative at home or in your job — no matter what your job is:

1. Change your patterns.

Go to lunch with someone different. Take your break at a different time or mix up the established pattern with which you do tasks. Routines are things we fall into because they save us energy over time. They are incredibly useful. But they also can be barriers to creative thinking. Try mixing it up!

2. Draw more.

Verbal processing is the grease of creative thinking. Talking out loud allows the tumblers to roll around till they fall into place in ways that couldn't happen otherwise. Likewise, drawing on a whiteboard is a form of visual processing that allows either a group or individual to see ideas, sequences, connection points, etc. Get a big whiteboard and put it somewhere where you'll use it. Or, if you're like me and think white boards are ugly, get a custom piece of frosted glass cut and mount it to your wall—not only will it function like a white board, but it's different and pleasing to the eye.

Start carrying a pen in your pocket. Draw on napkins at coffee shops and restaurants. Talk with your hands and use pictures to illustrate what you're saying. Visual aids double the creative clarity of communication.

3. Rediscover the mission.

Spend a day reflecting on the mission of your job.

Revisit the mission statement.

Try to imagine what "mission accomplished" would look like and why it would matter.

Go around and ask others how they would describe the

mission of the company. Ask what motivates them. Ask what their favorite part of the job is. Ask the story of how they slowly found themselves in the place where they're at.

Fall in love with why you're doing what you're doing all over again. Creativity feeds on passion.

4. Create a history log.

Think of the best things you've done in your job or career. Make a list. Organize the list by either importance or value. Ask others what they've seen in or through you.

Reflect on your successes and be reminded of your contribution.

See your impact all in one place. Notice the trends. Realize what kind of creative or innovative ideas you typically bring. Learn where your creativity lies.

Spend some time dreaming if there is a second iteration to something you've created in the past. Since we're most intimately acquainted with the things we've created ourselves, we often have the best chance of finding additional possibilities or ways to further what we've begun by continuing to focus on or develop them.

Dream about whether you could duplicate the things you've created in another market space if you made a change. You may be the creative answer to another company if you can establish the connection or figure out how to bridge ideas into a different context.

5. Speed up interactions.

Creativity ends up being innovative most often as it begins to touch and involve others. Speed up these connection points. Affirm ideas. Nothing speeds up the rate of interaction in a workspace or home more than when people begin to anticipate and expect affirmation.

Make work fun. Smile. Create energy.

Shut down your computer and walk around. Change the scenery. Change the music.

Inspiration rarely happens when we're sitting around waiting for it. Inspiration shows herself to the courters who pursue her hardest.

Creativity Is Something You Carry

Remember, you can create. I know this because you are *made* to create. It's how you were designed. As Ron Carter so beautifully put it, "Creativity is not simply a property of exceptional people but an exceptional property of all people."[3]

The list of things you create, and can create, is infinite. Ultimately, it's about learning that *creativity is something you carry with you as you move through time.*

The past might be painful, the present might be challenging, and the future might look daunting, but you can create.

The call to create and innovate shouldn't feel like pressure to perform a creative act or accomplish something massive. Rather, creativity is about our natural human responsibility and desires. The best parts of who we are, and the things we care about the most, are the things with which God has creatively gifted us. Our job is not to constantly achieve brand-new results that are unsustainable, but rather to maintain the steady mindset of a creator.

When we open ourselves up to creativity, even in small and seemingly mundane situations, we are giving life to the image of God within us. And as we'll see in the next chapter, which discusses the third part of our theology of creativity, we are called to do this for the sake of the world.

For further study at KenWytsma.com

1. 10 Ways to Be More Creative
2. 3 Prayers for Trusting God in Times of Struggle
3. Raising Creative and Confident Children

Questions for Group, Team, or Individual Reflection

1. List and discuss five ways you see creativity in everyday life.
2. What are three things you could do now to plan for greater creativity this year?
3. How is confidence in God's providence connected to the freedom to be creative? What are the challenges you see in bridging trust in God to creativity in life?

Chapter 3

Redemptive Creativity

The past is our definition. We may strive with good reason to escape it, or to escape what is bad in it. But we will escape it only by adding something better to it.

Wendell Berry

In the theology of creativity we're discussing, we've seen that God created, creates, and will create—and that we join Him in that process as people made in His creative image. Creativity matters so much, in fact, that it's part of our DNA as children of God. If that's true, what is God's end game in populating our planet with creative beings? In other words, *why* create?

Making Space for Life

This question was on my mind while attending The Justice Conference in Australia, where I met Wynand de Kock, a man who has spent decades thinking about exactly that. In his 50s, Wynand is South African by birth but lives in Melbourne now. He fought against the racial policies of South Africa toward the end of apartheid and, as an educator incredibly gifted at creating educational curriculum and models, developed what is known as the Open Seminary System.

As both an educator and an artist, he too has thought deeply about a theology of creativity, and he has an insightful idea about God's creativity based on Genesis 1:1–10. He believes that God's primary creative act was to *separate* light and dark and the heavens and the earth—all before bringing life into being. In other words, God's first act or impulse of creativity, like an artist preparing a canvas, is to make space for life. Real, physical space.

As Wynand writes, "When I think about God and what He is passionate about, one of the first things that comes to my mind is that He makes space for people to know His life-giving presence. God makes space for life, space in which we can engage him."[1]

What an amazing way of articulating the *telos,* or goal, of creativity: *Make space for life to flourish.*

That is what innovation and creativity do. In fact, that is what all of us are called to do: make space for life.

For Wynand, innovation takes the form of creative justice. To illustrate, he draws a parallel from the ability to make space for life to the importance of land rights. Wynand is deeply involved in advocating for the Aboriginal people of Australia, who are facing many of the same challenges that arose for those oppressed by apartheid in South Africa. In South Africa, the townships kept whites and blacks separate; in Australia, Aborigines have been (and continue to be) forcibly removed from their land. Justice allows or protects space for people to flourish. In contrast, injustice deprives people of the ability or space to flourish. Land is such an important topic in justice issues because to remove land is to remove life, to kill potential. Whereas when the relationship between land and people is properly ordered, land *is* space for life. For example, when God liberated the Israelites from slavery and injustice under Pharaoh, He established them in the Promised Land for security and the ability to flourish. Land, or space to live, is essential for a full understanding of justice.

OUR CREATIVITY most closely approximates **GOD'S CREATIVITY** when our ultimate purposes align with His.

Another illustration connecting creativity and health comes from the use of various art forms in treating victims of trauma—especially children. Drawing, playing, storytelling, and creating in general is increasingly proving essential in helping trauma victims process narratives, communicate wounds, and work toward healing.

We can also see the connection between making space for life and age-old human vocations. A politician who helps govern a city is entrusted with a broader responsibility to make space for life. The flourishing of a city, which in ancient Greece was called the *polis*, is really at the heart of what *politics* and *policy* are about (both coming from the Greek *polis* and by definition aiming at the good of the city). Those who govern, and the systems and structures they put in place, are supposed to allow for the flourishing of the city.

The home, too, is to be a space for life to flourish. Parents prioritize family dinners; they enforce chores to keep the house habitable; they decorate, plan activities, and seek to capitalize on teachable moments. They work budgets, run errands, and pursue the family's safety and comfort. All the way from the Golden Retriever to the guests who come and stay, parents seek to create an environment that encourages nurture and growth.

The success of the pastor or shepherd, as evidenced in the Good Shepherd passage of the gospel of John (chapter 10), is measured by the health or flourishing of the flock. Even leadership, in this sense, has a creative component; leaders have the responsibility (or opportunity) to make space for life and nurture those in their charge. When nonprofit leaders, pastors, and entrepreneurs demonstrate the best of creative leadership, they create space for health and flourishing in their organizations and institutions.

This is also why it's such a complicated issue when our foods and goods result from a system that involves exploitation. Unjust systems require people who aren't given space enough for healthy living to in turn provide the stuff we require to make space for life on our end. The ethical irony is striking: we can be, unknowingly, making space for *our* life by taking space from others.

God's creativity—and ours—is one of the primary vehicles God uses for us to find, develop, or make the space to flourish. Perhaps now, more than ever, we need to recapture a biblical perspective on the aim of creative energy.

Redemptive Creativity

God's ongoing creativity has an infinite number of implications for both who we are and what we do. In other words, God's creativity informs much of our sense of identity and purpose.

Take memories for instance. Memories have the power to stamp identity in people. My focus on making space for life within my family and community drives an intentionally creative focus on making memories. I try hard to create experiences that, as a family, we can hang on the timeline of our life. As a pastor of a church and a leader of a staff, I've begun to realize making memories is an important part of my intentional creativity. Community isn't something we fall into. It isn't something that just happens to us. It's something we forge. And we do it as we follow our creative God.

A fundamental part of Genesis 1:27—that God created men and women in His relational image—is that our similar creative capacity can be used to glorify God as we pursue justice and human flourishing within our relationships. We see this when we give life, affirm someone, lend a hand, or bring about goodness in any way. We see this in random acts of kindness. We also see this when we accept responsibility for things. All people at all times have the ability to bring about *change in the world*.

Changing the world is often a fuzzy idea in most justice conversations; there are idealists on one hand and pessimists on the other. The idealists think we can fix the world, while the pessimists think we can't and therefore shouldn't bother. Both are missing the point. Just because we can't fix the world doesn't mean we can't change it. The person who texts while driving and causes a crash that harms or kills someone, changes the world for the worse through destructive energy. Starting a nonprofit that brings education to girls in Eastern Congo changes the world for the better through constructive energy.

Mother Teresa changed the world. Steve Jobs changed the world. But we don't need to aim for that level. Every occupation can be creative in its own way. Our parents, teachers, and friends have all shaped, influenced, and changed our lives. My fourth grade teacher had a subtle—yet significant—impact on my life. He instilled in me a love for history, and what I do now when I teach at Kilns College is directly connected to his influence.

All of us influence someone—and as we exert that influence, we *all* change the world daily . . . for better or worse.

Making space for life—physical space, mental space, emotional space—gives a picture of how creativity is connected to the *positive* kind of change in the world—flourishing, goodness, and justice.

Creativity alone, for those who follow God, isn't sufficient. Not even ongoing creativity. Our creativity, like God's, must be aiming at something good. We need redemptive creativity—creativity that aims not just for success, but freedom; and not just for ourselves, but for others and for the good of creation as a whole.

Our creativity most closely approximates God's when our ultimate purposes align with His. Or, as my friend C. Christopher Smith puts it, "Creativity that is redemptive in the fullest possible sense is creativity that is driven by the imagination of the biblical reconciliation of all things."[2]

It is this end or goal—utilizing creativity to be agents of reconciliation in the world—that gives us a standard or criteria for evaluating our creative ideas and pursuits.

We can summarize the theology of creativity we've been building in three parts:

> 1. We are all creative, made in the image of a Creator God.
>
> 2. Creativity is an ongoing process through time.
>
> 3. Creativity is aimed at making space for life to flourish.

In our creativity, our intent needs to match God's: to make space for life to happen, for goodness to take root, for fruit to be borne, and for God to be glorified. When that happens our creativity is aligning with God's image in us.

In part 2 we'll explore more thoroughly the practical side of these theological tenets, but I want to offer a sneak peek here and introduce the context where the practical and theological work together in our lives. Here are the terms we'll be building on in future chapters, each one a counterpart to the tenets above:

> 1. Imagination (our ability to dream, envision, and hope for better realities).

2. Intentional Creativity (the discipline of creating and putting legs to imagination).

3. Innovation (a successful redemptive paradigm shift or culture change resulting from applied creativity).

The diagram below illustrates how the theological connects and bridges to the practical. In many ways it is the map of this book:

You may be wondering how this illustration connects to your life. At the heart of this book is the connection between the theology of creativity and the application of that creativity. I see its most relevant application in what I call "narrowing horizons," areas of life where change feels unwelcomed, unnerving, and insurmountable.

Narrowing Horizons

Change has a way of taking away our certainty, security, and control, leaving us feeling anxious and powerless. The more things change—or the narrower our horizons become—the more we feel anxious and powerless, or *the less space we have for life to flourish*.

So what do you do with that? Let's return to the Second Law of Thermodynamics and the concept of closed systems.

Our rapidly changing culture can give us a feeling of narrowing possibility. Take for example a business where the market is shifting. Or a church that finds itself living in a very different post-Christian climate than when it was founded three decades ago. Or a nonprofit realizing the next generation won't contribute charitably as much as the previous generation did (leaving it exposed and its sustainability in question). Or, lastly, think of teachers who face not only changing educational models and expectations for how they run their classrooms, but very different generations of students with more challenging home structures, new technologies, and a whole different way of responding to or respecting authority in the class.

This epitomizes the closed system with entropy and diminishing horizons. It is characterized by decay, fear, and hopelessness. If we drew a diagram of narrowing horizons, it would look like this:

It's in that moment of anxiety or panic, when the possibilities seem to have dried up and we feel hemmed in on all sides, that there is the greatest possibility for *making space for life*.

It's also when there is the greatest need.

I recently saw a great example of this in the animated film *Big Hero 6*. (When you have four daughters spanning seven years, animated movies are a godsend for whole-family activities.)

In the beginning of the movie, the youthful protagonist, Hiro, is trying to think of an invention that can land him in a prestigious school for gifted engineers. Completely stumped, he is about to give up—until his older brother grabs him by the legs and holds him upside down.

> "What are you doing?!" Hiro asks.

> "Shake things up! Use that big brain of yours to think your way out," his brother says.

> "What?"

> "Look for a new angle!"

Hiro looks and, seeing his project upside down, suddenly has a breakthrough idea.

Later, at the film's climax, Hiro and his team of teenage prodigies are fighting a villain—and losing. There seems to be no way out. Then Hiro remembers his brother's advice and relays it to the team: "Look for a new angle!" As soon as they view their narrow problem as an opportunity, it takes only seconds for each member—assessing his or her surroundings, special gear, and talents—to see an escape route where they hadn't before, and soon all of them are back working together to fight the villain.

Like Hiro and his team, our greatest motivation to make space comes when we're out of room. (Ironically, it is often the sheer *size* of our world that can make us feel trapped.) But it is at that moment of narrowed possibilities, when we're most tempted to slump our shoulders and do what we've always done, that creativity and innovation can open up new horizons.

And though we can't predict exactly when we'll need to innovate, we can be prepared when the moment comes. You can see it like an equation:

> *A narrowing horizon*
> *(a context/problem requiring a solution)*
>
> +
>
> *Intentional creativity*
> *(a pattern of life emerging from a nourished imagination)*
>
> =
>
> *Innovation*

This process is organic, not calculated. But those who are primed to innovate are those who make intentional creativity a habit of life.

Expanding Horizons

If our drawing of narrowing horizons is expanded with the possibility of creativity, we could draw the entire process of innovation like so:

Intentional creativity means harnessing the image of God in us, bringing hope and newness of life and space to flourish.

In 2008 a group of us at Antioch entered into a relationship with World Relief to start an innovative project called World Relief NEXT. World Relief is a sixty-year-old organization born as an evangelical disaster relief organization following World War II. Currently they work in dozens of countries around the world, providing relief in disaster situations and working toward sustainable development in emerging contexts.

For some time Dan Brose and Stephan Bauman, then the senior vice president of programs, had been watching the changing currents in the relief and development space. The advent of mass communication and the Internet, the ease of travel brought on by post–Cold War globalization, and the emerging awareness of social justice issues created an explosion of nonprofit organizations. Statistically, roughly 90 percent of the nonprofits in the world were created in the last decade or so. That's mindboggling!

This proliferation of nonprofits presented challenges—diminished horizons—for established organizations like World Relief. It increased the competition for charitable donations and grants. It also created a very confusing market space for average Americans to know the difference between a new organization with shallow roots and an established one, like World Relief, with deep roots.

Dan and Stephan realized that as an older organization, they needed to innovate to better connect with donors and be able to tell their story in a more compelling and effective way. If not, World Relief would become the best-kept secret—an organization doing phenomenal work but lacking the ability to effectively enlist people to join in their work.

With the help of Dan and Stephan, World Relief NEXT was created. It was a kind of research and development operation located in Bend, OR, one of the most creative and entrepreneurial cities in America.[3] Over the course of the next three years, World Relief NEXT assisted in innovating World Relief's approach to churches, helping to illuminate them as more than communities that could pray or donate, but also as creative communities with God-given gifts and resources that could be creatively leveraged in support of various development projects around the world. Some churches have money, but other churches have artists, networks, hospitality, etc. World Relief believed that all churches had God-given gifts that could be beneficial if creatively connected to the mission of helping vulnerable people.

World Relief NEXT also led the charge in creating media resources and telling the story of war-torn Eastern Congo to the broader evangelical church. The conflict in Eastern Congo had largely gone unnoticed by the church in America until that point, even though it had claimed the lives of an estimated 5.4 million people. The Congo advocacy campaign included not only events and video projects, but also a full-length collaborative music project and album called *The Congo Benefit Project*.

Even the end of World Relief NEXT brought life. The project's end led to successive creative endeavors emerging from the same creative movement and people. What began as a volunteer-driven, innovative project became an integrated part of the World Relief organization when they opened a creative office in Bend called the Bend Creative Team. This team also played a creative role in the birth and formation of The Justice Conference.

In many ways, what Dan Brose and Stephan Bauman (who became the president and CEO of World Relief) did was exemplify the very creative process we've been espousing.

Confronted with diminishing horizons (like fundraising challenges), they imagined what could be, acted on the creative impulse, and ultimately brought to life an innovative model that not only revitalized a large established organization, but was directly responsible for everything that came downstream: Congo campaigns, a Haiti relief project, and ultimately The Justice Conference itself. They looked for a new angle, and now men and women in Hong Kong, Australia, the States—and soon Holland, New Zealand, and South Africa—are learning about justice and being inspired to give their lives away—a generation impacted for justice because a few creative and innovative people responded to God and were willing to take a risk!

Imagination and intentional creativity, aimed at making space for life, resulted in innovation. This is the kind of story that drives me to write this book. The world is changing, and there are constant challenges, but God made us creative and has told us where to aim.

We are not hopeless as we peer out upon narrowing horizons; we are empowered.

Look Ahead

All of us breathe things into existence every day that didn't beforehand exist in this world. We are all creators. Creativity is a mindset of imagination and potential. It takes the building blocks of today and uses them to make space and expand horizons for tomorrow.

We may not be able to fix the world, but we *can* change it. We can't slow or stop the technological explosion we are currently experiencing, but we can learn to harness it for good.

I'm not saying all of your life should suddenly be one hundred percent creative. (Parents with children in diapers or students of calculus know that much of life is mundane.) But just as adding one painting to a bare wall changes and animates your home, a creative mindset alters everything. A little creativity makes all the difference.

In the face of narrowing horizons, we can look instead into expanding horizons. We *will* find ourselves in places where possibility seems cut off. We'll be laid off from a job, or lose someone, or move. The entropy of life happens. And then, all of a sudden, we will see an opportunity opening before us.

It is in us—as a gift from God—to do this. And our understanding of God's end goals in His creative work—the health and flourishing of all creation—gives us a place to stand whereby we can discern, judge, and commit to creative and redemptive pursuits.

The future requires *intentional* creativity as we make space for life and seek the reconciliation of all things.

Soon we'll explore further how to practice intentional creativity, but first let's take a look at just how much the world is changing—because it's changing too fast for us *not* to be creative.

For further study at KenWytsma.com

1. VIDEO: Humility and Art
2. VIDEO: The Congo Benefit Project
3. Blog Interview: Wynand de Kock

Questions for Group, Team, or Individual Reflection

1. Where are you experiencing narrowing horizons in your life or business? Do a speed brainstorm, imagining how impending life change could also serve as a catalyst for something new.
2. What are areas where Wynand's "making space for life" mantra helps clarify purpose for you?
3. Name three changes in your life you've been contemplating but have resisted because of fear of the unknown. Commit to seeking advice and praying about engaging the one that feels most significant.

#CreatevsCopy

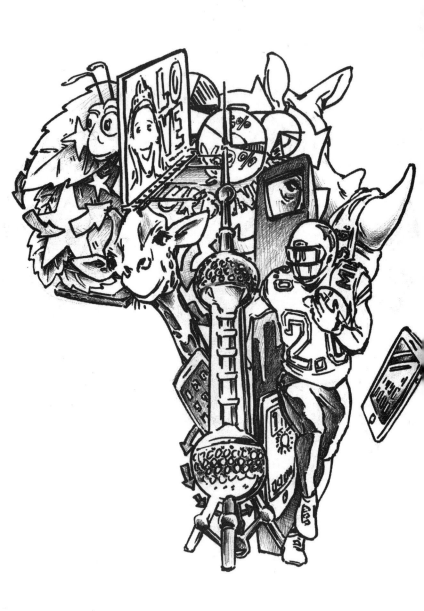

Chapter 4

Expanding Horizons

You need chaos in your soul to give birth to a dancing star.

Friedrich Nietzsche, *Thus Spoke Zarathustra*

My daughters and I recently watched *A Bug's Life*—one of the earlier Pixar Animation movies. In the opening sequence, a line of ants are carrying food in a long line across the ground. Suddenly a giant leaf floats slowly down from above and lands directly in the path of the ants, cutting the line in two. Immediately the ants behind the leaf start stacking up like cars on a Southern California freeway.

One of the sergeant ants spies the situation from afar, hands his clipboard away, and runs down the hill to the scene of the traffic jam. Very gently, he starts guiding the first worker ant around the leaf while slowly and pedantically chanting, "Around the leaf. Around the leaf." He stays for a moment as one by one the ants caught behind the leaf begin to follow in the new path . . . all to his slow, rhythmic "A-r-o-u-n-d the leaf."

I think this is a great picture of what can often happen to us.

Change occurs. We panic.

The world turns. We freeze.

Challenges arise. We all begin stacking up.

And to all of this, the creative spirit needs to sing, "Around the leaf."

Money problems? "Around the leaf."

Work challenges? "Around the leaf."

Relational disappointments? "Around the leaf."

Globalization? "Around the leaf."

We have within us the power to adapt. We possess the Spirit of the creative God within us. We can imagine new solutions. We can innovate. We can move out together on new paths and explore distant horizons.

We don't have to be defeated.

We don't have to copy.

We can create and move around the leaf.

Creativity in a Changing World

Recently my friend Tim showed me two pictures that absolutely shocked me.

Tim is a tall, good-natured guy with a big smile. His quiet confidence instantly puts you at ease, and you'd never guess that he's an executive at one of the most important banks in the United States—Silicon Valley Bank—overseeing all their foreign branches. With his finger on the pulse of venture capital and tech startups in London, Tel Aviv, Mumbai, and Shanghai, Tim has an incredible vantage point on the leading edge of globalization and global change. He spent the last several years living in Shanghai, helping open the first 50/50 joint venture in banking between a US bank and a Chinese bank (with the Chinese government owning half and Silicon Valley Bank the other half).

We were chatting about globalization when Tim showed me how much Shanghai has changed. The first picture he showed me was Shanghai in 1990, and the second was taken from the same vantage point today—less than twenty-five years later:

Tim asked me, "How much has the Boston skyline changed in the last twenty-five years? Or London? Or Chicago? When you

compare Shanghai's growth rate to growth rates of other major cities, it's as if the entire metropolis popped up overnight—like a whole Manhattan!"

Study the pictures page left. You can see exactly what Tim was saying—skyscrapers on the scale of Manhattan popping into existence from one image to the next.

When Tim first showed me this, it blew my mind! And it still does.

Sometimes the rate at which the world is changing escapes us. Once I was kayaking across Crescent Lake in central Oregon, frustrated, thinking I was making zero progress with a strong wind in my face—until I changed my perspective, that is, and looked at the shore. While staring across the lake gave me the sense of no movement, looking aside to the shore and seeing the fast moving treeline showed me how quickly I was actually moving through the water.

The dizzying speed at which the world is changing is a huge deal. Think of the number of problems that have arisen in that curve of the river in Shanghai in less than a generation! But those problems are opportunities to innovate.

Change can be exciting, frightening, and frustrating all at the same time. But the simple truth is that communities, businesses, and churches have existed at every explosion of change that has occurred throughout human history. They have absorbed the invention of the printing press, the Eurasian discovery of the Western Hemisphere, the Industrial Revolution, two world wars, the nuclear bomb, and the Internet. Many different generations of humanity have weathered change.

We are not alone.

This isn't the first time the world has changed, and it won't be the last. But as with all change, if we're going to lead or steer culture, creativity, faith, justice, or business, we have to not only know about it, we have to understand it. This helps us *be out in front of it*. Learn how to adapt to change and innovate in the midst of it, or be left out of date and behind.

As we close the first part of this book, which has unfolded a theology of creativity, I'd like to share with you a conversation I had with a friend who lives at the intersection of this theology and its practice. He not only understands the changes in our world, but he gives us a wonderful model of what it means to adapt and innovate within these changes and provide space for life to flourish and God to be glorified.

A Case Study in Creativity: The New Africa

My friend Keith Wright, an accomplished innovator in his own right, understands well the realities of globalization. He's considered by many (including the federal government) an expert on doing business in Africa. Keith lived for many years in Central Africa and recently stepped down as president of Food for the Hungry, a global relief and development organization, to start Thrive Global, a consulting agency helping large organizations learn how to do business in Africa.

Keith was happy to share some insights with me for this book. Sitting over breakfast at a Portuguese cafe in Bend, I asked Keith how a pastor's kid from Paradise, Pennsylvania, ended up becoming an international leader in relief and development. His answer surprised me:

> *I'm one of five kids, three of which are intensely involved in international work. We grew up in a house that was internationally minded. My dad was a small town pastor but felt compelled to get involved internationally. He was an innovator in his way— his passion for the international community led him to invite fifteen Iranian Air Force officers who were stationed up the road into our home on weekends. It would be an understatement to say that was unusual behavior.*
>
> *After graduating from college, I heard about some friends that were working in rural Uganda, and I decided to spend some time there before law school. My first introduction to Africa was not shopping malls*

*and sushi in Nairobi; it was being the only English
speaker within a four-hour drive, living in a house
that I built—not very well—with a grass roof. I went
from middle-class suburbia to a year-long isolated
monastic experience . . . and almost went crazy.*

*When my time at the Ugandan cattle ranch was
over, I had three options: go to law school, play
rugby professionally in Australia, or stay in Uganda.
Perhaps surprisingly, I chose option three. Living
alone in a place where no one spoke my language,
I underwent a huge spiritual turnaround. I came
out of that experience very passionate about serving
the poor and, somehow, challenged by how to do
that effectively, because I realized something: it's not
enough to care.*

Thinking about his new position with Thrive Global, I asked,
"Why would Western companies want to get into Africa? Is
Africa really changing and developing that much?" His answer
startled me:

*Everything is changing in Africa. One out of four
people in the world will be African by 2050. Africa
will be the world's top producer of food in twenty or
thirty years. Many African countries have completely
leapfrogged over landline telephone networks and
gone straight to cell towers. Because of that, in areas*

where cellular technology is allowed to flourish,
more money moves through cell phones than through
formal banking. Africa is light-years ahead of the US
in technology facilitating sales through cell phones.

I could sense my perception of the future of Africa changing as we spoke, so I asked, "What's the biggest change you think is heading toward Africa?" He quickly replied, "Urbanization. For example, in Uganda we're predicting a 25 percent overall increase in population, but a 40 percent increase in how many people live in cities."

The shift from a rural culture to an urban culture is an enormous transformation. It's a night and day difference. And if Keith was right, it was occurring throughout Africa as we spoke. I had to ask, "What does that change for you, as a leader, an innovator, and someone who cares deeply about the continent?"

I've been involved in Africa for 22 years, and while
I first went to change the continent, for the last five
years I've been wrestling with some of the changes
that are shaping it. In my opinion, Africa is the new
China, and that means we have to begin adjusting
the way we approach it. We have to stop thinking
that the solutions to Africa's problems involve
sending thousands of white people there to fix it. We
have to stop thinking that Western money, Western
business, and Western workers need to go there and

*patch up broken, poverty-stricken communities. We
need to realize that many areas in Africa don't need
a hand up—they're already standing on their own,
and some of them are ready to run.*

*The most efficient use of a dollar to change a country
anywhere—not just Africa—is to build a road from
A to B. In other words, the most effective way to
impact a country is to create infrastructure (health
clinics, cell phone networks, etc.). Fair trade coffee is
a good thing, but it doesn't have the economic thrust
or long-term potential of an electrical grid.*

*What that meant for me was that it's time to get
out of the relief and development world and
begin fostering local business, infrastructure, and
employment in Africa. Entrepreneurs always have
to make a choice between being connectors or being
creators, and I decided to be a connector, which is
what our company Thrive Global is. Our informal
tagline is "Leveraging Africa's strengths," and our
goal is to accelerate good ideas, good people, and good
capital in this very new, very dynamic environment.*

As a pastor, president of a justice-focused college, and a speaker
on biblical justice, I know hundreds of people who are
involved in nonprofit work in Africa. What Keith was saying was
troubling. If relief and development is becoming an outdated,

ineffective way to approach Africa—if they are leading to diminished horizons, in other words—then many of my friends and colleagues have some serious cultural turbulence ahead of them. I couldn't resist asking, "What does all of that mean for nonprofits and relief workers?" He answered resolutely,

> *Diversify or die. If you're dependent solely on sponsorship, grants, or private funding, you're in trouble. Good nonprofits learn to get proficient at all the different methods of fundraising. There are also new opportunities to raise funds locally. Now nonprofits are beginning to raise funds within the countries they are trying to help. Instead of sending a check from Granny to Guatemala, let's ask Miss Guatemala to be our spokesperson, buy up some of the billboards in the capital city, and get the wealthy there to raise money for their own poor.*

What a picture: Miss Guatemala with her pageant smile and wave, imploring people to embrace God's call to love their neighbor. And why not? Have we been bound by an America-can-do-it mindset so strongly that our thoughts on world change have only been wrapped up with *us* as the agents of change?

Keith's words are prophetic. Instead of seeing ourselves as the ones bringing change, we can open our eyes to a world of possibility that we can empower, collaborate with, or join.

*Everyone working in Africa needs to fall in love
with change. Human beings don't sit still. ISIS is a
scary, destructive movement. The lightbulb was a
life-giving invention. There's something in us that
wants to create and push things to the next level.
We constantly aspire for different, even though it's
not always better. During my time at Food for the
Hungry, I loved being open to how the world was
changing, specifically on the continent of Africa.
That love is what led me into my current career.
I'd rather embrace change than run away from it
or try to keep doing things the way they've always
been done.*

Those words really hit me. Not all of us are gifted with Keith's adventurous personality. For those of us who don't *naturally* make gutsy decisions like turning down a spot on an Australian rugby team to work on a ranch in rural Uganda, it's *difficult* to embrace change! I should actually say it this way: it's *natural* for us to resist change. None of us really enjoy adjusting to new sleep schedules, receiving new instructions for doing something we've already learned how to do, or adapting to changes in our office relationships. Unless something makes us really miserable, we'd rather keep things the way they are.

Change is uncomfortable. Change is unfamiliar. But change is unrelenting, even outside of Africa.

I realized I had just stumbled upon one of Keith's innate strengths. He knows how to make change his ally, rather than his enemy. I like to try to absorb my friends' superpowers when I can, so I asked, "What's the secret to surviving change?"

Innovation. Yesterday's solutions already don't work. The first step of innovation is hitting refresh on all your assumptions, and if you fail to do that, you become outmoded quickly. The middle class in Africa grew by 15 million in five years. Eighty-four percent of people in Africa use cell phones, but only twenty-five percent have access to power. If businesses aren't paying attention to the cultural shift in Africa, how will they ever compete in such a rapidly transforming part of the world?

What I'm trying to say is, pay attention, be humble about what you think you know, and be ready to change the way you think, operate, and view the world.

To use a rugby analogy, much of what we're doing when we innovate is trying to pass to where the receiver's going to be. Using the same analogy, the pass might be perfect, but the receiver can still trip and fall, or the pass can be intercepted. No matter a culture's trajectory, unpredictable forces like famine, drought, terrorism, and natural disasters will always have to be taken into account. The more we've

*developed a habit of innovation, flexibility, and
creativity, the better equipped we will be to deal with
surprises.*

I dug a little deeper. "But it can't be as simple as being on your
toes and allowing what you do to change all the time. Isn't consistency important? Isn't momentum over time important?"
Keith was ready with an answer:

*Of course! That's the trick—making sure the ways
you're adapting make sense and line up with what
you're trying to accomplish. If you want to change
culture, you can't allow it to dictate terms. Pick
your priorities and keep them small. If you want
to change or innovate within an organization, you
need to have narrowed down your goals and know
what you are trying to accomplish. Failure to clarify
the mission will lead to wasted time, wasted energy,
and a failure to establish any long-term momentum.*

*As for consistency, successful innovation is built on
best practices. I'm not saying we should change for
change's sake.*

Quickly shifting gears into a strong leadership tone, Keith
continued:

Some people celebrate or embrace anything that's

new or different, rather than narrowing their focus
to the innovative ideas that are built on strong
fundamentals. Just because something has been done
before or done in a certain way before, doesn't mean
it should be rejected, especially if it was successful.
The best innovation often builds on successful
patterns and practices from the past.

I reflected on those words for a second and then repeated them back, "The best innovation often builds on successful patterns and practices from the past." This underscored the point I've tried to make before, that the creative mindset sometimes borrows ideas as solid building blocks on the path of innovation. Keith completed the thought by adding:

You can innovate your way out of business if you
embrace innovation for its own sake. Innovation
without taking the relevant data into account will
run a business into the ground.

Accepting the cultural shift that precipitates the need for innovation is almost as important as the need and desire for innovation itself. That's one message we need to absorb from Keith—a fearless expectation and engagement with change. Not only do cultural shifts create a need for innovation, but they impact and transform the context and platforms from which we pursue change.

I thought back to my meeting with Tim Hardin and some things he mentioned about the loss of *cultural identity* through globalization, which tied into this point of changing contexts. Tim had asked,

> *What does that mean for learning or educating? If you're a pastor, how does that knowledge shape your ministry? If you're a businessperson, the implications can be profound. Companies aren't thinking about geographic markets anymore. To some degree, almost every field is going to have to grapple with the loss of geographic identity and the new globalized world.*

Tim's comment that almost every field is going to have to grapple with the loss of geographic identity (and the resulting complications and anxieties) could almost have been the problem statement that precipitated this book. "Innovation," he concluded, "is the only rational response for anyone who wants to have a say in how the future plays out. If you aren't out in front of the change that's occurring, solving problems and creating new solutions, no one will listen to anything you have to say, and you'll quickly be left behind."

We can't live a theology of creativity in a vacuum. Our understanding of the globalized world in which we live is essential for a practical and well-lived creative response to the unique challenges and opportunities we face.

The first step of innovation is
HITTING REFRESH
on all your assumptions.

When I talk to groups of leaders on creativity, I describe a belief that leadership used to be more focused on effectiveness—good communication of vision, strong teams, healthy processes, etc. It's a lot like coaching in the NFL and maximizing all that is needed to become more and more effective. I call this Leadership 1.0.

But what if the game kept changing? Not just new styles like the West Coast Offense or the Read Option, but what if the field dimensions changed, the number of players allowed on the field kept changing, and additional levels of fields were being routinely added? Then, in addition to effective leadership, creativity would be essential. I believe leadership is headed to a new level—what I call Leadership 2.0—that requires the coupling of creativity and effectiveness.

Creative leadership is what the future requires.

We might be able to see change and principles of innovation much better at a distance (like on the continent of Africa), but creativity works the same way in our lives and in our cities as we respond to the changes and opportunities presented to us. No matter where we are or what we're doing, innovation—as Keith said—means hitting refresh on all our assumptions.

We can strengthen our imaginations and pursue forms of redemptive creativity in the world as we steward our influence and become creative leaders.

Innovation Fatigue

When I think about the rapid rate of change in society and the need to be innovative and redemptive within it, I sometimes feel overwhelmed. It can feel like making art with a gun to my head—an image I was given by a friend who for years ran a commercial graphic design firm. Feeling pressured to create tends to rob us of the joy of creating. One of the hallmarks of human nature is that we eventually come to a position of fatigue and need a breath. Nothing is more debilitating than being told you need to innovate and change the world when you're already burned out. It's like hitting the shutdown button.

Innovation fatigue is why so many nonprofit leaders are stuck in desperate patterns of survival, endlessly reacting to the latest emergency or urgent trend. Often the best they can do in this state is copy other creatives and innovators. I have found myself—as a dad in my forties—in the same place. I feel like my startup energy is gone; my passion for creativity dried up. I have asked myself, "Am I hopelessly caught behind younger people who have fresher ideas and more time to pursue them?"

In a *Forbes* article, California-based neuropsychologist Rick Hanson, PhD, states, "Chronic stress degrades a long list of capabilities with regard to creativity and innovation."[1] Fast culture doesn't only make us stressed, but it seemingly cuts at our ability to be creative and adaptive. Slowing down, therefore, might not just be another way of combatting narrowing horizons, but one of the key strategies for safeguarding and nurturing our human creativity.

Slowing down can help our creativity, and our creativity can help us find better and slower rhythms for flourishing. We need to get enough sleep, we need to practice self-care, and we need to pace ourselves.

Embracing creativity is about leaning into who we are as children of a creative God, whose Spirit and power move in our lives as we respond to Him and endeavor to make space for life. A theology of creativity not only undergirds our practice of creativity, but it's what gives confidence and peace of mind as we work to innovate in our own context.

The realization that today's influencers must function in an innovative way isn't about demanding some kind of instantaneous result. We're not trying to go from zero to sixty in one breakthrough, heroic act, or campaign. It's about learning to move to a different rhythm, interpret data through a different filter, and evaluate structures and methods through a discipline of creativity.

I am optimistic. We can confidently pursue God's intentions for our life no matter our circumstances.

Generations of people following God have met the challenges of their day. We can too. We can imagine new solutions and find new ways to thrive. We *can* conquer anxiety by looking to the natural creativity that is ours by virtue of being made in the image of God.

Remember This

I realize that Keith and Tim are engaged at the upper level of global leadership and innovation. The point of their stories isn't to set an exceedingly high bar for our creativity—that it has to be global and in some upper level capacity few of us will reach. The point is to paint a clearer picture for us of how broadly and significantly the world is changing. You may be feeling only the ripples, but Keith and Tim are able to show us where the rocks are being thrown into the global pond.

Distilling their experiences into principles that can apply to everyday leaders like you and me—people who lead in churches, schools, businesses, ministries, and the home—here are a few things we can all learn:

1. The world is moving fast.

2. Change brings possibility.

3. Possibility is harnessed best when we're willing to risk and walk forward.

4. Walking forward, or being innovative, means we have to be willing to change as the world changes.

5. Change isn't natural, but it's something we can prioritize, plan for, and practice.

6. Innovation isn't the end; it is the means. Innovation serves higher ends.

As argued so far, our inherent creativity works through time as we adapt to change and pursue our calling to be agents of reconciliation in this world.

And, when all this gets overwhelming, see point #2 above and remember: Change brings *possibility*.

As we move now to part 2, we'll discuss the practice of creativity —the best way to respond to change and explore possibility.

For further study at KenWytsma.com

1. 3 Ways Relief and Development is Changing, by Stephan Bauman
2. The #1 Thing Every Nonprofit Must Do
3. 5 Documentary Recommendations for Understanding the World We Live In

Questions for Group, Team, or Individual Reflection

1. What stood out most to you about the interview with Keith?
2. What are the top three ways you've seen, experienced, or are dealing with rapid societal change?
3. Keith talked about the new rules or new conditions of international relief and development (such as valuing the experience of local talent and voices). What are some of the "new rules" you discern in/at your work, leisure, parenting, school, or church?
4. Are there ways you could apply some of Keith's principles of change in your sphere of influence?

#CreatevsCopy

Part 2

*In everything truth surpasses
the imitation and copy.*
Cicero

*Man is never truly himself
except when he is actively
creating something.*
Dorothy Sayers

Pra
Cre

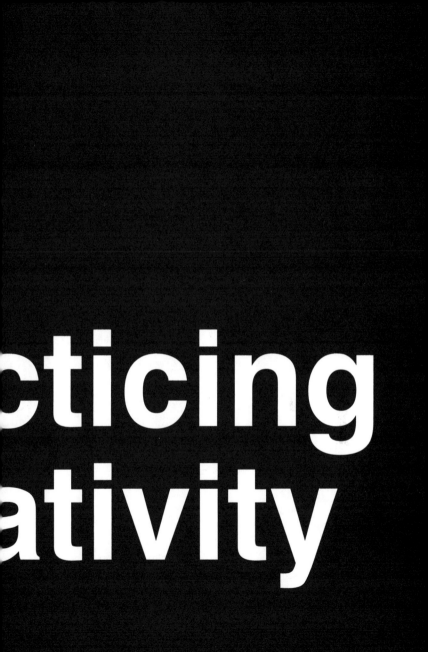

cticing
ativity

Chapter 5 Recapturing Our Imagination

You can't depend on your eyes when your imagination is out of focus.

Mark Twain, *A Connecticut Yankee in King Arthur's Court*

By now you may be feeling both excited and nervous about creativity.

I know I am. We now turn our attention to the actual *practice* of creativity. The best place to start is the furnace of creativity: imagination.

Imagination

Copernicus served for forty years as the canon at the Cathedral of Frombork in his native Poland, what he called one of the remotest places on earth. There he dreamed up a heliocentric (sun-centered) vision of the universe using only imagination and mathematics. The telescope that would be so useful to Galileo decades later had yet to be invented. Copernicus said this about coming upon his discovery:

> *For a long time I reflected on the confusion in the astronomical traditions concerning the derivation of the motion of the spheres of the Universe. I began to be annoyed that the philosophers had discovered no sure scheme for the movements of the machinery of the world, created for our sake by the best and most systematic Artist of all. Therefore, I began to consider the mobility of the Earth, and even though the idea seemed absurd, nevertheless I knew others before me had been granted the freedom to* imagine *any circles whatsoever for explaining heavenly phenomena.*[1]

It was through imagination that Copernicus came upon his great discovery. Similarly, Einstein spent his time as a clerk dreaming and doodling ideas that would eventually become his theories of relativity. J. K. Rowling was fired from a secretary position because she spent so much time thinking up a little story about a boy named Harry Potter.

What do all these people—and you—have in common?

One incredibly important word: *imagination*.

If creativity is part of the image of God in us, imagination is the divine spark that unleashes it. Imagination is where creativity, innovation, and all truly new and original work begins. This is why we must recapture our imagination. Who better to inspire our dreaming than one of the most imaginative authors of modern times, C. S. Lewis?

Imagination and Story

One of the reasons I love C. S. Lewis and many of the writers he associated with is that they argued for imagination and the value of fairy tales, which stand as symbols of imagination in its purest, childlike form.

For C. S. Lewis, what we would call the real world is, in many ways, less real than the world of fantasy.

For example, if I pointed out the window right now and passionately began talking about the aspen tree that started as a seed; was nurtured by soil, water, and sunlight; grew year after year from something no bigger than a seedling to a forty-foot-high sentinel; and now somehow knows when to shake off its leaves and then get dressed again every year, wouldn't that sound a lot like more like magic than the way we typically talk about trees?

In the minds of people like Lewis, Tolkien, and G. K. Chesterton, the language of fantasy often better approximates reality than other literary forms. If fantasy doesn't better *approximate* reality, then, at the very least, it might often be the best genre for getting at or *explaining* reality. In Lewis's essay "On Three Ways of Writing for Children," the reason for writing children's stories that most applied to him is that "a children's story is the best art-form for something you have to say."[2] Perhaps this is one reason Jesus spoke in parables: He understood that saying in story what He could have said plainly had a greater effect, that it *felt* truer, that it spoke through the mind and into the heart.

In C. S. Lewis's own parable of sorts, *The Great Divorce*, he explores the qualitative difference between heaven and earth. Lewis viewed earth as the "Shadowlands," which lack the solidity and stark reality of a robust heaven. Those on the edges of heaven, still getting used to its ultimate reality, are more like ghosts than humans. As creatures not fully established into the heavenly realities (made solid), they can be cut by the blades of grass or pounded by drops of water—both being more solid and complete than they are. To me, this is some of the most beautiful imagery in literature. It's our imagination that allows us to wake from the dullness of simple perception and behold the magic and mystery of reality. In other words, imagination keeps us from taking reality for granted, from seeing normal as boring. An aspen tree becomes a life, not just vegetation.

Taking this one step further: imagination not only helps us see

Imagination not only helps us see more clearly what is, but **WHAT SHOULD BE.**

more clearly what is, but *should* be. Again, Jesus' parables illustrate this. We are angry at the debtor forgiven of much who won't even forgive little. We are moved by the father who slaughters the fattened calf for his prodigal son. We are challenged by the parable of the Good Samaritan. We come away eager to practice forgiveness, grace, and mercy. The prophet Nathan's famous parable of the rich man who slaughtered a poor man's only sheep (illustrating David's sins toward Bathsheba and Uriah) makes us outraged by the injustices of theft, adultery, and murder. Nathan could have simply said, "David, you sinned greatly," but he used a story to shout it, and David fell to pieces in repentance.

C. S. Lewis was once asked in a letter by a mother what to do about her son who had fallen in love with the character Aslan, a lion symbolizing Jesus in The Chronicles of Narnia, and wasn't interested much in Jesus Himself.

Lewis's response is telling of the healthy and strategic role of imagination in the formation of children. He counseled the mother not to worry at all, that what her son loved in Aslan wasn't the lion, but the character and traits of Jesus he had empathized with. Lewis confidently wrote that as her son aged, the external form of the lion would fade and the love for the heart of Jesus would remain strong and refined.

Imagination was allowing her child to go much deeper into the heart of Jesus than artists' renditions of Him in children's Bibles would allow for. In fact, the child could go deeper than do the many adults who hold in mind a tame, placid version of Jesus. For as Lewis was able to show with Aslan, Jesus is "no tame lion."

For Lewis, children see life more as it really is, before the enchantment of pride and the dullness of age take hold. His hope was that the process of maturity would return us to childlike wonder at some point. That we would one day wake up and be able to see the magic in the trees and recognize that the forest is indeed enchanted. This is illustrated in his precious dedication of *The Lion, The Witch, and The Wardrobe* to his goddaughter:

> *My Dear Lucy,*
>
> *I wrote this story for you, but when I began it I had
> not realized that girls grow quicker than books. As
> a result you are already too old for fairy tales, and
> by the time it is printed and bound you will be older*

still. But some day you will be old enough to start reading fairy tales again. You can then take it down from some upper shelf, dust it, and tell me what you think of it. I shall probably be too deaf to hear, and too old to understand a word you say, but I shall still be your affectionate Godfather,

C. S. Lewis[3]

*But some day you will be **old enough** to start reading fairy tales again.* Isn't that thought provoking?

The Test of Imagination

G. K. Chesterton helps us explore the magic of imagination even further. In the tales and myths told to children, he saw—like Lewis—the values that allowed such an exuberant view of life, something he called the "test of imagination."[4] Fairytale laws are often arbitrary or nonsensical—and children have no problem accepting them. A tree that bears fruit of silver or gold, a magic berry that opens ears to the chatter of animals, or a mirror that declares the fairest of all—these are nonsense in real life, but accepted as hard fact for the sake of the story. A strange law—the frog will only turn back into a prince with a kiss—is created solely for the story, and it works. Fairy tales make sense, not only because they follow a certain logic, but because they also invent a logic of their own whenever necessary. That's part of their magic.

And this magic breaks into real life. You can see it in the way children invent games, rules, and stories with each other when they play; they create and inhabit worlds at the same time. In "The Ethics of Elfland," an essay about the value of children's fantasy, Chesterton observes that a life filled with excitement and dreams is not only more fun to live, but it also tends to be more accurate. The poetry of life is always there. As Chesterton says, "The vision is always a fact. It is the reality that is often a fraud."[5]

Sadly, as we grow older we slowly calcify and increasingly fail the test of imagination. We lose elasticity; our imagination has a harder time escaping our circumstances to dream new realities. Another way of saying this is to discuss what has been called our *social imagination*. Social imagination is a way of describing how our creativity is usually bound or constrained by our culture and peer group. We typically dream inside these artificial boundaries and rarely escape the social imagination to fully dream or bring ideas to bear created solely for our story or in response to God's call on our life.

Divergent Thinking

In a talk for the Royal Society for the Encouragement of the Arts, Manufactures and Commerce, creativity expert Sir Ken

Robinson illustrates this with a longitudinal study (recurring over time) on the occurrence of divergent thinking. Divergent thinking isn't the same thing as creativity, which Robinson defines as "the process of having original ideas that have value."[6] Divergent thinking is an essential component of creativity, however, because it's the capacity to interpret a question in multiple ways or imagine multiple answers to the same question.

In the study Robinson cites, sociologists asked 1,500 kindergarteners this question: "How many uses are there for a paperclip?" Where many people answer with 10–15 examples, those who are good at this (genius level) are able to provide 200 or so examples. They'll think imaginatively, "What if the paperclip was as large as a building?" or "What if the paperclip could float?" The results of this study and the decline in divergent thinking over time are shocking:

> *The first tests were given when the children were between three and five years of age. Ninety-eight percent of the children scored in the genius category. When these same children took identical tests five years later, only 32 percent scored that high. Five years later it was down to 10 percent. Two hundred thousand adults over the age of twenty-five have taken the same tests. Only 2 percent scored at the genius level.*[7]

The study shows two things clearly: we all inherently have the capacity for creativity, and it typically declines or deteriorates over time.

Robinson attributes the results to modern education and standardization around Enlightenment values, where creativity and the arts generally get pushed to the bottom of the pile.

After dealing with the real world so long, we get stuck inside the parameters we encounter. We lose our ability to accept that crazy ideas and big dreams are possible. We become standardized and learn that wrong answers are bad. We stop dreaming and don't try for fear of failure. Surprise and wonder become things of the past.

One of the problems I deal with as a pastor is the challenge of prayer. I find that many Christians struggle with or are disappointed with prayer. Their experience has left them confused, disillusioned, or jaded toward the notion that God responds to our requests.

I've come to believe that our problem with prayer is connected to our problem with divergent thinking. When we ask for something in prayer, it's usually very specific—money, for example.

We typically don't address the root of our request—that I feel insecure, I'm worried about caring for my family, that money is a resource needed to fulfill my calling, etc. We simply pray for the thing we imagine will fix our problems.

Our expectation for an answer from God is bounded by our request. If we receive money, God answered our prayer. If we don't receive money, God didn't answer our prayer and we come to feel prayer doesn't work.

Divergent thinking, however, allows us to better understand our needs as well as envision a multitude of ways God might address our need for security, provision, and resourcing. With an open imagination, we're better able to see the subtle and inventive ways God continually moves to guide and care for us. We *see* God answering our prayers.

Jesus spoke often of people not having the eyes to see what God was doing. He chose young disciples (arguably most of Jesus' apostles were teenagers) and described them and others as young wineskins able to adapt and grow with His teaching as opposed to many of the religious leaders, who were more like old wineskins that had lost their elasticity or religious imagination.

Divergent thinking and imaginative capacity is not just an artistic aptitude or a valuable business asset; it is also a deeply spiritual quality.

Growing Young

Picasso once said, "All children are artists. The problem," he continued, "is how to remain an artist when they grow up."

Imagination, it seems, has a lot to do with inspiration, freedom to dream, and an appreciation for wonder.

So rather than respond to many of the stresses of today from a creative standpoint, we labor in an arbitrarily small universe bound by lack of imagination.

But perhaps it doesn't have to be this way.

As Sir Ken Anderson argued, "We are born creative and it is worked out of us."[8] Creativity, like most human capacities, is a muscle that can either atrophy or grow through exercise.

With imagination, the old can learn to grow young again. Put another way, when it comes to our capacity to imagine, we need to mature out of adulthood.

This is the world I believe Christ is calling us to inhabit. This is a big part of the secret of contentment and the ability not to worry about the future. The future isn't determined, and our problems aren't bigger than the ability of the God who dresses the flowers and feeds the birds.

In a magic world we create. In a magic world we dream.

In a magic world, copying is for those who have eyes but cannot see and ears but cannot hear.

Imagination is far more powerful than we think, and it isn't just for children and fantasy authors.

If we want to be creative, we must cultivate our imaginations. Read children's fantasy. Put down *The Times* and thumb through *Winnie the Pooh*. Paint with your child. Doodle in church. Watch BBC's Planet Earth. Stare at the clouds. Shut off Excel and go outside. Take a walk in the woods.

If we want to grow young, we have to play, dream, explore. There is magic in the world, if we have the eyes to see it.

For further study at KenWytsma.com

1. Book interview with Walter Brueggemann on *The Prophetic Imagination* and *Sabbath as Resistance*
2. 10 Ways to Be More Creative
3. Book interview with Jerry Root, the C. S. Lewis scholar behind *The Surprising Imagination of C. S. Lewis* (coauthored with Mark Neal)

Questions for Group, Team, or Individual Reflection

1. What are some ways you have seen that "adult" thinking is actually a duller, less realistic way of viewing reality than the imaginative eyes of children?
2. Sunsets, friends over meals, smiles, or words of affirmation: make a list of three areas of simple beauty like these that you would like to focus on more this week as an exercise in reawakening wonder and imagination in your life.
3. Imagination and divergent thinking can have a beneficial effect on prayer. What are other areas of life you believe would benefit from a greater ability to think divergently?

#CreatevsCopy

Chapter 6 Imagination and Innovation

I saw an angel in the marble and carved until I set him free.

Michelangelo

Imagination is not just whimsical; it is intensely practical.

Unleashing imagination is like starting a campfire the old-fashioned way. Strike the flint against a stone and it creates sparks. Not all the sparks set the tinder ablaze. Usually you have to strike the flint repeatedly. But in the end, a few of those sparks will begin to burn, starting the first flames that will lead to a full fire.

Imagination and the Creative Process

Imagination allows us to thrive instead of stagnate, but we have to understand its role in the creative process. We have to be willing to treat it like flint, and wait for the right sparks.

Here's a diagram that shows how imagination relates to innovation.

Notice the stages where imagination plays a key role. Scholars have worked for years to classify imagination based on the roles it plays in dreams, planning, situational awareness, and much more.

Quickly, here are three basic types of imagination we use to find solutions—comprehensive, artistic, and practical imagination.

> *Comprehensive imagination*. This is the ability to think about the situation, mull over the data and the problems

presented, comprehend the facts at hand, and fit them together to build a complete picture of what's happening. At this point many people turn to diagrams, lists, and doodles to work out their thoughts with the help of physical media. It's a very simple type of imagination, but it forms the *foundation* of the innovative process. Mistakes in this type of imagination lead to a poor understanding of the situation at hand—and usually stagnation. Do you have a sufficient grasp of the challenges you're facing? How would you represent the landscape at home or work if you drew it on paper for someone else? Who do you think could help you gain a clearer picture of the challenges and opportunities in front of you before you start thinking through solutions and strategies?

Artistic imagination. This is what many people think of when they think of using the imagination. This type of imagination is closely related to creating new ideas. When a poet dreams up a new poem or a musician writes a new tune, this is the artistic imagination at work. But it goes beyond the fine arts. When a marketer thinks of new brand content or a parent tells a new story to her kids, artistic imagination is at work. It is how we dream. It's how we interact artistically with the world, and all of us can learn to do it! Many of us do it naturally as parents or teachers without realizing it.

Artistic imagination can also be successfully applied to the here and now. It's what people use to think of new scenarios, picture new possibilities, imagine what *could be* out of what *is*. Employing this type of imagination, we develop ideas, art, and possibilities previously unconsidered—sparks on the tinder. Artistic imagination is the stage where a myriad of new ideas are created, though only a few of them are destined to survive.

Practical imagination. This is the imagination that looks at all the ideas and dreams up a solution that can really work. It's a more goal-oriented form of thought. Practical imagination looks at the current state of reality and the problems presented, and then it looks at the ideas created using earlier types of imagination.

This might sound silly, but recently my wife, Tamara, addressed a growing problem—first world problem, for sure!—in our house. When we take trips, we like to take pictures. For someone who believes life is about making memories, pictures are a wonderful tool. Often, especially with kids, a picture deepens or even *becomes* the memory. We pick our favorites and hang them on the walls in our house. However, with hundreds of leftover pictures piled in stacks around the house, we felt like we were missing out on many of our memories. My wife found a Hallmark card display rack in an antique store and decided to order two of them for our house. We now have card racks in our entryway and in our living room, proudly holding dozens of stacks and thousands of random family and trip pictures. Our kids, and our guests, sit in a space holding the fullness of who we are and telling our life story, whether they're flipping through pictures or just subconsciously aware of them in the background. That's an example of practical imagination dreaming up a workable solution.

As you can see, imagination—far from being frivolous or childish—is immensely practical, and it might be one of the most powerful aspects of being human. During an interview in 1929, *The Saturday Evening Post* asked Albert Einstein, "Then you trust more to your imagination than to your knowledge?" Einstein responded: "I am enough of the artist to draw freely upon my imagination. Imagination is more important than knowledge. Knowledge is limited. Imagination encircles the world."[1]

Sit there for a second. *Imagination encircles the world.* Nearly everything you see began with an idea. The chair you're sitting on; someone thought it and made it. The paintings on your wall; those are the result of imagination and raw material. Your job (or the one you're applying for) exists because a company imagined a project and the personnel needed to complete it, and your job was part of their design. Hundreds of satellites encircle the earth, and they wouldn't exist apart from imagination. There is no innovation without imagination.

Imagination as Re-imagination

A big part of imagination is re-imagination—rethinking paradigms and innovating accordingly. One of my favorite re-imagination stories is that of Kilns College, where I teach and serve as president. At Kilns I work alongside a small group of committed, hardworking individuals who are willing—and eager—to think creatively.

In 2008 the Kilns College administrators made a commitment to stand apart from the traditional higher education model, to imagine other possibilities. There are thousands of institutions of higher education in the United States alone, so rather than being a small fish in a very big, very established, very traditional pond, we decided to imagine what was beyond that pond—what others either hadn't dared to do or lacked the space to create fully.

In a system of higher education that charges upwards of $50,000 per year for tuition, we imagined what it could look like to cut that number not in half, not thirds, not even quarters, but down to nearly a fifth of the average tuition cost. Today, with limited overhead, Kilns College operates distinctly outside the reality of most institutions, and we're free to imagine, dream, and create, to focus every dollar on *truly* engaging students in their learning experience.

Kilns College thrives by offering degrees other institutions rarely have the opportunity to imagine. Degrees that are needed now. Programs that serve students in the present. Topics and issues that individuals can engage while they are current and relevant. We're throwing deteriorating learning models out the window and opening a world of possibilities in their place. Using a flipped classroom model (more on this in a bit), and a practical project-based thesis component, the college can take a new degree program—such as our Master of Arts in Innovation & Leadership—from conception to reality in less than ten months.

Today, many graduate schools are forced to operate in an insular environment, limiting the learning experience to the voices and expertise readily available on campus. Kilns, however, thrives on authentic collaboration. We are working with partner organizations from Southern California to Raleigh to Hong Kong to bring a global array of opportunities and faculty voices to students. We do this while simultaneously serving the needs of our partner organizations and their communities.

Kilns College is re-imagining how to provide first-rate education in a fluid, mobile, globalized culture. And as a result of that creativity, we are seeing the lives of students change in places we never dreamed of.

Two Challenges to Imagination

I don't want to make it sound like embracing imagination and accepting new ideas is always an easy, trial-free process. It isn't. Two specific challenges come to mind.

The first challenge is knowing when ideas—even those with plenty of momentum—need to be laid to rest.

Linguists have a category called "clipping." Clipping is what happens when a word or phrase, like *mobile vulgatus* ("mobile peasants"), gets shortened ("mob"). It's how *fanatic* becomes *fan* and *caravan, van.*

I see the work of imagination and its result the same way. Often we must travel the full circuit of the creative process in order to find the simple clipped nuggets of practical value—the ideas that work, the flashes of insight, the projects worth investing in, etc. Along the way we may come up with a host of seemingly great ideas, but not all of them will make the cut.

There's a popular literary quote that says, "In writing, you have to kill your darlings."[2] In other words, be willing to sacrifice the characters, plots, scenes, and settings that you love the most for the good of the overall story and greatest emotional impact. The "kill your darlings" advice often applies to the world of projects and programs.

Steve Jobs once talked about how the secret to creativity at

Apple came in what they said no to. "I'm actually as proud of the things we haven't done as the things we have done. Innovation is saying no to 1,000 things."[3] Pruning is as much a part of the creative process as planting. Part of creativity is choosing what to leave behind in order to move ahead.

Another challenge of imagination is convincing others that imagination isn't relegated to just a few people. Everyone has some capacity for imagination, and that capacity can be discovered, nurtured, and put into practice. And it *must* be put into practice if we are to follow the call of our creative God.

Some are good at recognizing this within themselves, and those with a high capacity are quickly recognized as creatives. Others struggle to recognize their capacity for imagination but can create amazing ideas when encouraged. Still others may have a relatively low capacity for imagination, although they may excel at encouraging creativity in peers and taking care of other details—activities that benefit immensely from what imagination they do employ.

IMAGINATION
is not just whimsical; it is
INTENSELY PRACTICAL.

Wherever we are on the spectrum, we *all* have the capacity for imagination, and we can all grow that capacity—all of us. Whether in business or family, work projects or relationships, it takes commitment to recognize we can overcome our problems with imaginative thinking.

Flipping the Classroom

One of my favorite stories of creativity—one that illustrates the imaginative process well—is that of Aaron Sams.

Aaron was one of my groomsmen. We became friends while I was a grad student and he was in college. Aaron and I both shared a passion for education as well as creative thinking, and dreamed of collaborating on education models in the future.

Our careers took us separate directions after we graduated and both got married. I ended up in Bend and Aaron ended up as a high school chemistry teacher in Colorado. We reconnected, by chance, in early 2013 in Pittsburgh. I learned that Aaron had indeed found a way to effect change in education models.

In 2006 Aaron had taken a teaching job in Woodland Park, Colorado, where he met Jon Bergmann, another high school chemistry teacher.

Aaron and Jon began to discuss the problems of teaching high school science—the endless lectures, demos, and labs. Additionally, due to the remote location of their school, many student athletes would miss a lot of classes. They observed how the classroom seemed to address the easy stuff, while the harder stuff was left for students to do at home—as if school was using time and space backward.

With the increased access to the Internet and the advent of easy video viewing platforms like YouTube, Aaron and Jon began to experiment with recording the lectures for at-home viewing and reserving classroom time for the more difficult cognitive tasks.

Removing the lectures or demonstrations from class time forced them to rethink their approach. Aaron says they asked questions like, "What's the value of class time?" or "Why would anyone want to show up to my class?"

By swapping what was slotted for home and what was reserved for classroom, Aaron and Jon were able to dive deep. Amazingly, students started creating projects and products on their own. Instead of making the teacher happy or aiming at grades, students became passionate and curious about the subject.

Aaron and Jon didn't know they were spearheading a revolution in education. In fact, they didn't even know what to call what they were doing.

In September 2010, work and management author Daniel Pink wrote an article highlighting Karl Fisch, an acquaintance of

Aaron and Jon who had been interacting with and learning from them. Pink dubbed this new approach to classroom education taking America by storm "The Fisch Flip."[4] As a result of this article and a TED Talk referring to these innovations, everyone started calling it "Flipped Learning" or "Flipped Classroom."

Aaron and Jon now travel the globe teaching school districts in America and teachers in other countries how to create their own content and take control of their teaching environment. There are over thirty thousand educators in an online learning community, and the Flipped Learning Network hosts an annual conference helping teachers innovate in their approach to educating students on a variety of subjects. Where implemented, teachers are more satisfied and student stress and anxiety have gone down.

Aaron says he was simply trying to meet the needs of his students: "We saw a challenge to overcome and I saw some tools and imagined how we could use them." That *we* is important; as Aaron notes, "The collaborative aspect of it was huge; I wouldn't have done it on my own."

A Redemptive and Beautiful Response

Aaron and Jon's story highlights much of what this book aims at: a response to change, thinking imaginatively, being passionate about vocation, creating space for others, and the value of working collaboratively toward new horizons.

When we fix something, we are helping to turn death to life. Bringing order out of chaos. That is God's call to creators. To us. A redemptive and beautiful response to the challenges of life.

The word *create* comes from the Latin *crescere*, which, according to Merriam-Webster, means "to bring into existence (e.g., *God created the heaven and the earth*), to produce or bring about something, or *to produce through imaginative skill*." We all produce, and if creativity is the application of "imaginative skill," it is certainly open to anyone willing to give it their time, energy, and attention.

As a leader, you can encourage creativity in those you care for and create a culture of imagination. People need to understand that it's okay to dream—to envision what *could be*. Imagination needs to be coded into our behavior and environment.

May we remember that imagination is one of the highest forms of our humanity. As C. S. Lewis said, may we all grow old enough to read fairy tales once again.

For further study at KenWytsma.com ↗

1. Contemporary Trends in Education
2. Why Distance Education Makes Further Schooling Worth Considering
3. 3 TED Talks on the Science of Creativity

Questions for Group, Team, or Individual Reflection

1. What are some ideas you've had or challenges you're facing that are relevant to the three types of imagination (comprehensive, artistic, and practical) mentioned in the beginning of the chapter?

2. If you are a part of a team, what are some ways imagination can be nurtured in constructive ways in your work environment—from office décor, to planning meetings, to snacks, to strategic planning?

3. Take something from work or home and spend a few minutes thinking how it could be "flipped." Write or discuss some of your ideas.

#CreatevsCopy

Chapter 7

Intentional Creativity

Inspiration usually comes during work, rather than before it.

Madeleine L'Engle

It's hard to turn a parked car.

I thought about this one time while sitting in a parking lot watching a child in a car yank the steering wheel to and fro. It was a harmless exercise—the car wasn't moving, so all the steering wheel represented for the mom was a toy to distract the child.

Just like it's hard to turn a parked car, it's hard to innovate from a standstill. Most bright ideas don't fall from the heavens; they take shape over time. It took several years for Kilns to get where it is, and Aaron and Jon's process was full of trial and error. Neither story would have developed if the people involved didn't *intend* to develop something. The bridge between imagination (dreaming up what could be) and innovation (implementing the dream) is intentional creativity. How do you move across that bridge? You practice movement and alignment.

Thinking back to the child in the car, his steering didn't matter because he wasn't moving. But if the car were moving one, ten, twenty miles per hour, the steering wheel would have had a radically different importance. The same is the case with creativity.

Intentional creativity is forward momentum thoughtfully guided. Let's take up the first part of this equation: movement.

Movement

Starting is the first step in movement. Unfortunately, starting is always the hardest step.

Like getting out of bed in the morning, starting the base of a snowman, or breaking camp before getting back on the trail, the beginning is the begrudging work.

Simply put, we love our comfort; it's easier to stay put. Very few of us enjoy change.

Our natural response to change is to buck against it, to dig in our heels, to wish things would stay the way they are or go back to the way they used to be. It's nothing to be ashamed of; it's just how we are.

But the truth is, we don't have that luxury. Thinking back to what I said earlier about open and closed systems, our systems—jobs, families, companies, ministries, etc.—will dissipate if we build boundaries around them and close them off to change. We have to remain open and we have to move. The positive side is that it feels good to move. Marathon runners tell me that they often look at their long-run training days with a sense of reluctance, but eight to nine miles in they are feeling loose, relaxed, and centered, and they come home feeling energized. Getting out the door was worth it because the movement felt good. Getting things started with Antioch when it was a church plant was exhausting, but as momentum built it was energizing and brought with it a sense of deep satisfaction.

You might be thinking, "Yeah, I agree; change and movement are worth the effort, but I don't have the energy at this point in life to make it work."

I think we all understand that emotion and have all been there. In chapter 5 I said that creativity, like most human capacities, is a muscle that can atrophy or grow through exercise. Becoming more creative or prioritizing intentional creativity isn't something that happens overnight. Rather, it's a decision we make, a course we set, a value we commit to that allows us, our teams, or our communities to steadily become more creative over time. It begins with small steps.

There is research conducted by psychologist Robert Epstein showing that *strengthening four core skill sets* can increase the rate of new idea generation. In fact, over an eight month period, 55 percent of those tested showed an improvement in idea generation or demonstrated creativity.[1]

A 55 percent increase in demonstrated creativity is amazing! If the idea of becoming more creative excites you, but the process seems daunting, Epstein's four disciplines or skills could be a welcome roadmap or routine.

The four core skills Epstein recommends are:

Capture your new ideas.

When you have a thought, write it down. Grab whatever you can! Use the notes feature on your iPhone or Android. Talk your thoughts into a voice recorder. Keep a pad of paper on your nightstand. There is a story of the hit song "I Can't Get No Satisfaction," by the Rolling Stones.[2] Guitarist Keith Richards supposedly woke up one morning with a hangover and a recording he didn't remember making of a new guitar riff in the middle of the night. The memorable guitar piece quickly evolved into one of the band's biggest and most memorable songs.

Maybe we shouldn't copy everything about Keith Richards,

but capturing creative insight in the moment is a sure way to catalyze creative energy and movement.

Seek out challenging tasks.

Work on projects other people have failed at. Seek out questions that don't have an answer (or easy answers). Forcing your brain to work on challenging puzzles with nothing personally at stake can be fun and imaginative.

Try reading philosophy (which never seems to fully answer questions) or force yourself to figure out how to pack lighter and use less luggage. Think of a way to bless or encourage someone you don't like; this necessarily pits emotions and values against each other while producing a healthy outcome (assuming you follow through on blessing your enemy).

Broaden your knowledge.

Take a new class. Learn a new language. Visit a new city. Take music lessons.

With the Internet and the increasing amount of travel videos and instructional courses, there are more ways than ever before to explore new areas of knowledge. Start watching a TED Talk per week or download a college course from The Teaching Company, one of my favorite innovative education providers. Start slow and pick something you can succeed at. Overestimating what we are able to do only deflates and discourages us. Pick just one thing for starters. If you want to take on more later, you'll know it's working.

Surround yourself with interesting things and people.

Host dinner parties. Be creative with whom you invite to your dinner parties. Obtain question starter games for dinner tables and use them with your company to generate meaningful and broad dialog. Go to the opera, a dog park, or an art museum. Basically, be intentional about finding yourself in different crowds with different values and passions.

Epstein's steps remind us that creativity not only comes from imagination and focusing on problems, but also from creative habits and disciplines that keep our minds fresh. "As strange as it sounds, creativity can become a habit," says creativity researcher Jonathan Plucker, PhD, a psychology professor at Indiana University. "Making it one helps you become more productive."[3]

Movement feeds creativity, and vice versa. Active people seem to grow increasingly active.

So get started.

Tinker.

Create.

Scrap your ideas and then start over.

Share ideas with others—creative synergy is explosive. Plan for things to be messy. In early stages, value momentum as much as order.

Whatever you do, don't stand still—movement always wins over stagnation in the long run.

This applies to organizations, too. Don't be afraid to give people with strong artistic imaginations a voice. Uncreative organizations can be bogged down by their bureaucracy and fail to innovate, usually because practical, task-oriented leaders place little value on new ideas. Bad teachers stick to formulaic exercises and tired lectures that rarely engage students. Churches can spin their wheels on the same old ways of doing things until they run out of gas. If you want movement, be willing to let out the reins and allow creative and imaginative voices space to dream.

Alignment

With all of that said, movement without alignment soon becomes chaos.

Avoid unleashed, out-of-control creativity, especially in groups or teams. Fostering innovation is great, but if it isn't fostered within healthy constraints, you'll end up with lots of passion and little direction. Imagination struggles without end goals. Sparks may fly everywhere, but they will rarely find their way without order or conscious direction.

To navigate between the extremes of idleness and chaos, a reliable process must be established. You must find a way to encourage new ideas that neither kill innovation nor let creativity run wild. Seeking this balance requires a method of inputting ideas, like structured brainstorming or an idea-collection method. This acts as a filtering mechanism, a way of gathering and analyzing ideas then narrowing them down to ideal choices. Here is where those with practical imaginations are intensely helpful; they have a talent for managing both sides and effecting change.

INNOVATION
is the hard-won realization
of something that began as
IMAGINATION.

This is why large corporations often have research and development departments. It is far easier for those tinkering to have freedom at the early stages without interference, and it is far more effective for manufacturing to be able to focus on production without constant change or having to deal with the early up-and-down stages of hammering out ideas. In nonprofit organizations that run lean and can't afford research and development staff, creating space on the calendar for employees to wear different hats and exercise creativity becomes important. For individuals, travel and outside interaction such as conferences, study leave, or site visits may prove helpful. Innovative sparks often come from getting outside one's normal work environment.

Setting constraints is one aspect of alignment, but so is having an end goal. Whatever your end goal is—be it as general as "grow our church" or specific as "ethically provide high-quality, affordable backpacks to children of low-income communities"—it should fall within the redemptive role of creativity: making space for life. Making space for life is a core principle that runs through the mission statement of most groups and organizations. Every family, church, business, or nonprofit is— hopefully—trying to make space for life in some way. Every healthy system has an embedded mandate or mission connected to human flourishing. Our mission, our art, our creativity, the way we tell our story, or the way we sing our song—all of these should be deeply connected and aligned to an understanding of our role in God's creative, redemptive work.

I love when families have clear alignment. Tamara and I have an entrepreneurial friend named Tsh Oxenreider (yes, it's spelled Tsh) who is a big proponent of this. Tsh began a blog while living in Turkey with her family back in 2006, called *simplemom.net*, that quickly became a sensation and now continues as *theartofsimple.net*. It's one of the most successful creative- and simple-living blogs in the country.

Tsh teaches individuals and families how to clarify goals and simplify their lives. She and her husband, Kyle, developed the following values to help focus and shape their family culture:

> We will:
>
> - *Put each other first.*
>
> - *Cultivate deep relationships with one another.*
>
> - *Extend love to those around us.*
>
> - *Live simply.*
>
> - *Be true to who God made us.*
>
> - *Take care of our health.*
>
> - *Be good stewards of creation.*
>
> - *Be lifelong learners.*

I love the life-giving beauty of these phrases. Having refined and articulated a clear family vision and culture, they stand a much greater chance of accomplishing their goals and living intentionally—of moving forward together with aligned purpose.

When our kids were young, Tamara and I worked hard to boil down the values we wanted to build into our family culture. The challenge for Tamara and me was this: how do we instill nuanced behavioral patterns and decision-making skills in our kids without creating an impossibly complex matrix of rules and guidelines for them to absorb and follow? Because of their ages, we knew that we would have to come up with something simple, clear, and easy to define and understand.

We decided to start with the Ten Commandments, but ten seemed like too many, so we simplified them down to three (hopefully God won't be offended that we created an abridged version):

(1) Don't lie.

(2) Be responsible.

(3) It's better to give than to receive.

The goal was to create clear guidelines, because clear expectations beget clarity and confidence. If a playground is located next to a street and there is no fence, children will stay at the middle of the playground. If there's a fence alongside the street, children will play all the way at the edge of the grass, right next to the street.

Boundaries actually allow for life to flourish more fully. They define where we're allowed to be and where we're not. They free us.

The rules so positively impacted our family culture that we came up with a second set of three rules for vacation: (1) Don't whine, (2) Have fun, and (3) Be family. They define and make space for life in the car: you're not allowed to whine. And, yes, it's okay to have fun . . . but we do it together.

Our rules aren't perfect, and our family isn't perfect, but they've become a deeply personal success story of imagining what a healthy culture could look like in our family and finding methods to promote and reinforce those values in a fun and simple way.

Looking across the spectrum and finding core alignment in life, family, or business can help bring clarity.

Who are some people you admire, and what are their values? How would you translate these into a way that creatively meshes with your life and calling?

What is your goal and purpose as a student?

As a parent?

As a teacher?

As a retiree?

Why does God have you at the job you're at?

What is possible?

What's the big idea of what you're really trying to accomplish?

Be intentional. Then align your dreams and the fruit of your imagination with your efforts, time, and resources.

The process of aligning the important facets of life on paper often does the hard work of aligning and clarifying them in reality. So write them down. Then write action steps.

Innovation is the hard-won realization of something that began as imagination. Intentional creativity is the process that brings you through.

When our values guide our whole creative process—imagination, intentional creativity, and innovation—something beautiful happens. But the beauty will never come unless we get moving.

A Brighter Future

Innovation, the fruit of intentional creativity, is becoming a necessity to succeed over time as a leader or person of influence. We can lead or influence for a season without innovation, but if we don't innovate, switch gears, or re-create our game, at some point we will fall behind. Our information will be outdated, our strategies ineffective, and our sense of mission off target. If we want to be a person of influence who stewards God's gifts, creativity is a must.

When change in society happens as fast as it does these days, leaders must keep pace somehow. Through work, through passion, but also through creative adaptation.

In Keith's interview, he summed up the realities of today by saying, "Innovate or die." Innovate or die can be read as a heavy or discouraging message. You could be thinking, "I was already overwhelmed, and now I feel a greater sense of urgency along with one thousand more things I should be doing."

The point of this discussion, however, is not to bring guilt or to overwhelm. In fact, the opposite is true. I believe we *already* feel overwhelmed. Creativity, when we come to understand it as a human trait, allows us to look at the future, not with despair, but from a position of confidence and expectancy. Creativity isn't another thing to make us more anxious, but one of the ways *out of* anxiety!

The poet Maya Angelou once said, "You can't use up creativity. The more you use, the more you have."[4] Creativity snowballs into more creativity. If you are bogged down or feel stagnant, simply make a choice to start thinking about creativity.

Creativity can become a natural rhythm of life like breathing, eating, or sleeping. We can learn to innovate in response to the changing currents of today and the possibilities of tomorrow.

The challenges of today *can* turn from threatening realities to life-giving innovations... if we embrace our God-given creative potential. Every change, however unwanted, is an opportunity for God to move in our lives. Change creates opportunity to see God's creativity as well as manifest our own.

Instead of fearing change, welcome movement. Instead of becoming overwhelmed, align efforts. Instead of falling behind, create.

But we can't just create for creativity's sake; we must have a robust understanding of why we do it, of its ultimate aim. Otherwise we may waste our energy or even misuse it. For example, creativity and entrepreneurship have been tied to the more negative aspects of industrialization and capitalism that left social, racial, economic, and ecological injustices in their wake for much of the past two hundred years. If we aren't careful, we could regret our innovations.

So how do we decide and pass judgment on various creative acts? Is there a basis for evaluating or guiding creativity to constructive ends?

There is. It's to understand innovation and creativity as part of our redemptive calling in this world ... and that's where we're going next.

For further study at KenWytsma.com

1. 5 Questions to Ask Before Launching a Startup
2. 5 Ways to Increase Creativity in Parenting, by Tamara Wytsma
3. 3 Books on Intentional Living

Questions for Group, Team, or Individual Reflection

1. Does the phrase "Innovate or die" excite, scare, motivate, or discourage you? Why? Where in your life do you feel stagnant right now?
2. Look at the list of Core Creative Practices from this chapter. What is one thing you could successfully pursue in each category? (Consider building some dates and commitments into your calendar in order to get started.)
3. Choose 3 areas of life that are important to you—are they heading in a healthy and desirable direction? How could you practice alignment in these areas?

#CreatevsCopy

Chapter 8

Generous Creativity

Hospitality means primarily the creation of free space where the stranger can enter and become a friend instead of an enemy. Hospitality is not to change people, but to offer them space where change can take place.

Henri Nouwen, *Reaching Out*

Generous is a big word. It's oversized and I love it. Think of how many good things are related to the word *generous*. A generous raise, a generous slice of pie, a generous number of vacation days.

Generosity means plenty, and more than is strictly necessary.

Past the everyday examples, generosity is at the very heart of much of the goodness in our lives. Much of what makes life meaningful and enjoyable emanates from a generous spirit, while very little that is good can come from a critical or self-focused spirit.

Generosity is expansive, while selfishness is narrow.

Generous people bring others along with them, while self-absorbed people cut off community.

Generosity thinks big, even when thinking big is harder. Caring only about ourselves is simpler, but the ceiling is so much lower.

That's why I'm convinced there is no better way to sum up the theological and practical truth, goodness, and beauty of creativity than by calling it *generous creativity*.

As we close our discussion of creativity, I'd like to look at generous creativity through three key lenses.

1. Generous Creativity Is Collaborative

Generous creativity is collaborative because we all come from different starting points, *and we need each other to reach our full creative potential.*

One of the myths we tend to hold in society is that innovation results from one genius in a garage changing the world with radical inventions or new technologies, all alone. The truth is that at the heart of nearly every technological breakthrough, there's a team. Creativity and collaboration go together. Even all the way back at the start of the universe!

Genesis 1:26 reads, "Then God said, '**Let us** make mankind in our image.'" The Christian view of the Trinity means that creation comes out of a divine community. Collaboration is at the very heart of our Trinitarian view of God.

When best expressed, human creativity usually comes in a collaborative form. Individuals can dream, but it takes teams and partners to implement—e.g., Rodgers and Hammerstein, Jobs and Wozniak, Luther and Melanchthon, Susan B. Anthony and Cady Stanton, Michael Jordan and Scottie Pippen, the Coen brothers, Ben and Jerry, etc.

None of us are purely self-made or self-successful.

Most people give William Wilberforce the credit for abolishing slavery in England. He was the face of the abolition movement, especially in London, but he wasn't the founder of it. The earliest abolitionist document was written by Dutch and German Quakers in Pennsylvania, and the beginnings of the anti-slavery movement in England was formed when twelve men, not including Wilberforce, met at a print shop in London on May 22, 1787, and signed into existence The Society for the Abolition of the Slave Trade. While Wilberforce was one of abolitionism's greatest champions, he labored within a collaborative community.

Or consider the Inklings. C. S. Lewis, J. R. R. Tolkien, Charles Williams, and several other famous British authors banded together in a kind of literary club, reading their works aloud to each other in the 1930s and '40s. The Inklings didn't read to each other for entertainment, but for critique. Their creative disagreement and encouragement is one reason behind the success and enduring legacy of many of its authors.

To truly implement the things we imagine requires relationship, synergy, and creative friction.

Competition can be a very powerful positive motivator. I know because I'm competitive. Competition can also be something that undercuts creativity and collaboration. I remember one night eating with my pastor-friend Eugene Cho by the river in downtown Melbourne, Australia. It was late, we were jetlagged, and we'd been walking all day. As we sat down to eat, I found myself venting some thoughts about Christianity in America, thoughts that were really coming from a competitive spirit. It was only after the third time he changed the subject that I realized Eugene, in his humility, was steering me back to seeing things from a spirit of unity—a collaborative and synergistic space—rather than a competitive one. Venting is a mechanism for feeling good about ourselves. It might even prove that we've won over and against someone else, but it ultimately prevents *us* from winning.

Collaboration is how God created, and it is how generous creativity is best expressed. As Shane Claiborne so aptly states, "As Christians, we should be the best collaborators in the world. We should be quick to find unlikely allies and subversive friends, like Jesus did."[1]

2. Generous Creativity Is "In Process"

Since generous creativity is always collaborative—and always requires relationships—it should come as no surprise that it's never perfect. I'm choosing to use the positive side of that coin, and say it is "in process," but the meaning is the same.

Fortunately, there is a wealth of familiar examples that demonstrate perfection is often the *enemy* of creative innovation.

The French Renaissance landowner Michel de Montaigne (1533–1592) was the first to try a form of writing exploring short ideas while analyzing his own internal psychology. He called these his "Essays," which comes from the French *essayer*, "to try." Montaigne created a whole genre of literature by his project of trying to record creative—but imperfect, in-process—thoughts.

As Sir Ken Robinson says, "If you're not prepared to be wrong, you'll never come up with anything original."[2]

Some of the best plays in football are broken plays.

Some of the best comedy is improvisational.

Some of the best music is jazz.

Some of the best meals are variations on recipes.

And for many teams, the process of brainstorming or innovating—regardless of whether it leads to product breakthroughs—has unintended benefits:

- A reminder or deeper understanding of mission

- Greater relational interaction and appreciation of everyone's contributions

- A nurtured sense of creativity that bears fruit in the next meeting . . . or the time after

- Laughter and fun that reinvigorates morale and the workplace culture, because creativity flourishes where laughter is cultivated

Steve Jobs was famous for wanting perfection before products were shipped to market. I understand this and appreciate his attention to detail and desire for quality. But not all things we deal with can be as precisely tuned as a piece of electronics. Church and community development is always a work in progress. For example, when we started The Justice Conference, we used every relationship we had to line up speakers and artists who were willing to work for cheap or free to help make the vision a reality. We didn't have the kind of money that larger, established conferences had to pay honorariums.

In the end, however, this meant the final line-up on stage was less diverse than we would have liked. It was imperfect. As such, there were a lot of difficult conversations we went through during the following year with leaders who were concerned with the lack of diversity at the first event. As difficult as it was at the time, however, it has been one of the most redemptive and shaping experiences of my life. I met some amazing people and forged several lifelong friendships through the dialog, creative friction, and collaboration of that process.

Perhaps my favorite reminder that beauty and creativity don't require perfection comes from Michelangelo.

One of Michelangelo's most famous sculptures, the *David*, is housed in the Accademia Gallery, a nondescript museum with an entrance in a small back alley street in Florence, Italy.

There are two large exhibits at the Accademia—the Hall of the Prisoners (which houses the *David)* and the Hall of the Colossus. Upon entering the Hall of the Prisoners, you find yourself at the end of a long corridor lined on either side by several large sculptures. But you don't really see them, because the other end of the corridor opens into a brightly lit atrium, where the colossal, illuminated *David* sits underneath a specially designed skylight, drawing you forward like a magnet. Seeing the *David* for the first time is one of the most awe-inspiring moments I believe a person can have. It's that captivating.

Because of the majesty and perfection of the *David*, it's easy to miss the slabs of marble that line the Hall of the Prisoners. The slabs of marble are Michelangelo's *Prisoners* (or *Slaves*). They are part of a tomb project originally commissioned by Pope Julius II della Rovere, which was never completed.[3]

The *Slaves* are rough, unfinished pieces—human figures barely emerging from the marble. But as you look at them, they begin to come alive, as if they're struggling to free themselves from the stone. I remember thinking they were simply never completed, but I later learned that many art historians believe

Michelangelo intentionally left them unfinished. They possess a dynamic beauty that would have been lost had they been finished and perfected in the clean, precise manner of the *David*.

For Michelangelo, intentionality in one context meant completing the statue, and in another it meant leaving it "unfinished." The unfinished nature of these and other works by Michelangelo account for their power and magnetism. It's the strength of Michelangelo's vision, the intentionality behind his work, and the effectiveness of his process in aligning his vision with his art that make the *Slaves* so powerful.

Although they may have been finished in his mind, in appearance they look unfinished. I took away from his work the idea that not all of our creative pursuits have to come to a perfect end in order to be beautiful.

Things can be left unfinished. Maybe the *best* things are unfinished. And not all creativity has to be perfected to be beautiful.

3. Generous Creativity Is Redemptive

Creativity is not only about results; it's also about people. Creativity is often how we *demonstrate* passion or show others we value them.

Creativity is harder than duplication. It's easier to copy. Because copying is a shortcut, creativity communicates effort and concern—generosity.

We innately understand that creativity is intentional. So when we come to an environment when we can tell there is a value or a priority placed on creativity, we respect it. Somehow we know that someone is being generative and making space for us.

I've seen this most specifically in our own home. My wife loves to have people over to our home, and when she does she is passionate about them feeling loved. So when we have a dinner party, the food can't just be straightforward; she always puts a spin on it.

For example, every summer we have the Antioch Summer Internship Kickoff Barbeque at our house. It's never allowed to be a traditional barbeque. Usually it's a "make your own pizza" bar where newly acquainted interns have to pair up to make a joint pizza. And the ingredients aren't the normal fare; Tamara puts out a rainbow of vegetables, sauces, meats, and cheeses.

It doesn't seem like much, but people notice when you take the time to be more creative than Costco burgers, white buns, and standard potato chips.

There's a deep spiritual connection between the creative energy spent, and love received, in hospitality.

Creative people, as we explored in chapter 3, serve greater ends than their own. Like God's creativity, ours, too, is meant to be redemptive. A living or creative energy should fight for what's good, even when it's hard. As G.K. Chesterton writes in *The Everlasting Man,* "A dead thing can go with the stream, but only a living thing can go against it."[4]

That gets at the heart of both redemption and creativity. When God redeems, He breathes life into what was dead—and that is the eternal project to which we are called to lend our own creative efforts.

In fact, there is a connection between grace and generosity— they both involve sacrifice. Generous creativity declares that something outside of me has value. That I and my creativity somehow exist for something higher than myself—for the glory of God and the goodness of creation. That is why there is such a powerful connection between creativity and justice. If justice is what ought to exist when we have right relationships, creativity holds the power to elevate our thinking, draw us together, and call us back to just, hospitable, and generous living.

Sometimes this starts in acts of hope that seem too small to even *mean* anything, let alone *matter*.

I recently heard the story of Hiroko Fukuoka. Fukuoka is a Japanese woman who lives in the city of Scichigahama and walks the beaches to find remains from the tsunami that wreaked destruction along the coast of Japan in 2011. Fukuoka collects

Not all of our **CREATIVE PURSUITS** have to come to a perfect end in order to be **BEAUTIFUL.**

sea glass and other objects and turns them into jewelry. I saw her story first in the aptly titled short film *Finding Beauty in the Rubble*. Fukuoka first began collecting and making jewelry when the idea struck her while walking her dog, Kai, along the beaches. "Through creating this way," she says, "I get the feeling that I am not a helpless person."[5]

One of the typical responses to modern anxiety and the loss of control is to either seek power or to collapse our focus into ourselves. It's natural to redirect energy when you feel you are drowning. What I've been arguing, however, is that in anxiety and the loss of control we can turn to creativity rather than power. The move to creativity is a redemptive one. Instead of taking space, we create it. Instead of stagnating, we become innovators. Like Fukuoka, we give to others with a generous spirit, even if what we give is small.

Sometimes the problems in this world are very large, however. Often we don't understand why God allows dysfunction and inequity in society. We see beauty in Jesus' words concerning the kingdom of God, but we don't see it reflected in society. I believe much of this is because we are living lives that are less generous and less creative than they could be. Instead of living in faith as creative beings, we become individualistic.

Perhaps this is why the kingdom of God needs the church in order to become realized. We are designed to be a body—each part both receiving from and contributing to the others.

Creativity is many things, yes, *but it is also a love language.* The greater the redemptive love on our part, the greater the amount of energy we'll expend in making space for others. In short, we'll make greater effort at generous creativity. It is intrinsically tied to hospitality. This is the fullness of the theology of creativity expressing itself. It's the ultimate reconciliation of all things. Creativity isn't for its own sake . . . it fits within God's overarching plan.

"How, then, shall we create?"

You may feel like there is too much focus on imagination and doing things well—that it all feels too idealistic and heavy. If you're an overworked employee or bogged down with family commitments, the thought of rethinking life or undertaking a big overhaul to become more creative can feel like it's going to crash your system.

I have no desire to weigh anyone down.

The goal of a creative posture is that we might envision a future where we're more free and successful at doing what is meaningful and demonstrating love to those we care about. It is about opening up space, not creating short-term stress or adding pressure to life. Although stress can spur productivity in short bursts, there are many studies showing that stress is a well-known killer of creativity. Our goal here is not to add stress, but to alleviate it. Creativity can make space for rest. And in rest, creativity is renewed.

Creativity is also a journey. The goal is for it to become a deeper part of our life of faith. For faith, which is the opposite of walking by sight, can be nurtured and carried forward by a well-fed imagination.

Imagination is about flourishing, about vitality, about strength. Imagination, creativity, innovation—these are not esoteric skills that only a select few can practice. They are essential ways for each of us to interact with our challenging reality and pursue goodness and justice within God's creation.

Put back into a theology of creativity—a theology of life—we see that:

We are all creative.

Creativity is an ongoing endeavor through time.

And creativity is aimed at making space for life.

In short, we can aspire to *generous* creativity.

It is my prayer and hope that you—the imaginative, creative, innovative person God created—will activate your creativity. For your sake, for your family's and community's sake, and for the sake of the world.

For further study at KenWytsma.com

1. 3 Traits of Collaborative People
2. How to Grow through Failure
3. The Forgotten Art of Hospitality

Concluding Questions for Group, Team, or Individual Reflection

1. How would collaboration in your life lead to greater creativity and success? With whom could you collaborate?
2. What is an area where perfectionism or fear of messiness is keeping you from moving forward or creating something beautiful?
3. How would you rework your understanding of your personal, family, or business mission to make it truly generous and generative?

#CreatevsCopy

Conclusion

A New Song

Creativity of all kinds, in art, in prayer, in justice-making, in human relationships, is born where people wrestle with angels, outside Eden, on the border between heaven and earth, where they struggle to create a new form, a new song, a new template, a new ethic with all the discipline and passion they can bring to bear.

Kathy Galloway, *Dreaming of Eden*

Sing to the Lord a new song; sing to the Lord, all the earth.

Psalm 96:1

God commands us to sing a new song.

From the beginning, we were born to create. We are part of a grand creative process that began before we were born, has continued throughout our lives, and will be perfected someday in the future. It is our privilege and responsibility to make space for life, to breathe creativity into our world—in whatever capacity we can—so that life can flourish, even in the face of imminent change, grief, or death.

Don't Fear the Critic

As I shared in the introduction, I'm fond of saying there are two kinds of people in the world: those who *create* and those who *copy*.

However, the truth is there's a third type of person in the world: the critic.

Whereas the creator and the copier are both oriented toward progress, the critic is fundamentally against it. The critics (or cynics) find their satisfaction, not in trying to bring life, but in critiquing those who do. The creator seeks to walk on water. The copier prefers to wait for a dock. But the critic decides to stay in the boat. The negativity of the current situation is what gives him power.

The critic often sees new ideas as potentially dangerous or sees the risk in any unknown variable of new or innovative thinking. The critics are the anti-creators, the bystanders, the armchair quarterbacks, the people who kill motivation. I am reminded of the White Witch in *The Lion, the Witch, and the Wardrobe*, who infamously made Narnia "always winter, and never Christmas." The critic, likewise, lives in a gray world without the potential for change, where it's always winter, never Christmas.

Sometimes it's easier to slowly drown where we are at than to risk swimming to unknown locations.

It's easier for an established church to slowly die but be in full control than to allow creative innovation that feels out of control.

In the midst of all the change and anxiety, it's natural to find ourselves, at times, wanting to be the critic. It is, after all, a position that feels powerful. It's easy for the critic to be right, which is a cheap substitute for real change. When things seem beyond our comprehension or control, we can become rigid, cold, and cynical. It's a very human response to being overwhelmed, but it's one we must transcend.

Imagination is often what's required to lift us out of the gloomy spirit of fatalism into the clouds of positive thinking. Attitude and positivity are the forgotten wings of leadership. Nobody follows a cynic.

Imagination transports us from the world that is in front of us to the land of make-believe, to would-be worlds that hold within them tools and solutions needed for changing life below. Imagination, as it were, could be the mythic process whereby we receive fire from the gods.

I'm not saying we don't need critical thinking or discernment.

Good leaders will seek and embrace constructive feedback in the pursuit of innovation. But there is a distinction between criticism that prunes or refines and criticism that deflates, damages, or kills.

Critics happen. You can try to convert them, you can choose to ignore them, but you should never be afraid of them. Critics miss the point and refuse to work hard enough to keep up with the changing world—they take themselves out of the game. They have neglected their sacred calling to make space for life and, in some cases, are actively snuffing it out.

The critic pans for fool's gold and seeks a power incapable of beauty and restoration.

One of the hallmark stories of the Old Testament Israelites was that they continually preferred the idea of returning to the slavery they knew rather than taking the Promised Land they could only apprehend by imagination.

True power is found in trust. Trust believes God who was in control over the past is also in control over the present and the future. Life is found in recognizing creativity as a part of humanity.

What is more powerful than looking at the world through **EYES OF POSSIBILITY?**

How?

With *imagination*—our ability to dream, envision, and hope for better realities.

With *intentional creativity*—the discipline of creating and putting legs to imagination.

With *innovation*—a successful redemptive paradigm shift or culture change resulting from applied imagination.

It's necessary to dream, for the solutions of tomorrow often follow the inspiration of today.

Life to the Fullest

Like John Lennon said, "Imagine . . . it's easy if you try."[1]

Grow old enough to read fairy tales again.

Create. Don't copy.

Harness the power of imagination.

Find that place in life, in work, or in your family to see through a child's eyes. Children evoke the power of possibility—they live in a world unfettered, opened up by the freedom to use their creativity and say, "*Ah, but it could be this way.*"

What is more powerful than looking at the world through eyes of possibility? When we sing a new song—imagine new realities—we become participants in God's creative work, taking our place as co-creators with Him in this ever-changing, ever-messy but beautiful narrative.

If we are to live in a magic world with enchanted forests, we must be those who dream. We must be those who create.

The poet Elizabeth Barrett Browning wrote of our enchanted and spiritual world saying,

> *Earth's crammed with heaven,*
> *And every common bush afire with God;*
> *But only he who sees takes off his shoes;*
> *The rest sit round and pluck blackberries.*[2]

What I've hoped to do in this book is to open our eyes, not only to our God-given creative gifts, but to the possibilities that exist when we both see the magic in the world and are willing to harness our imaginations as creative leaders to bring forth all possible beauty.

Despite the changes happening in the world, if we see every bush afire, then maybe we'll see our ground as it is: sacred.

I wonder if Jesus espoused the faith of a child because in their minds good is still possible and endings can be happy.

Or maybe it's because the childlike posture is closest in nature to our ever-creating and imaginative God?

Maybe G. K. Chesterton summed it up best when he so poignantly argued for youthfulness of spirit. In one of my all-time favorite pieces of literature, he writes:

> *A child kicks his legs rhythmically through excess,*
> *not absence, of life. Because children have abounding*
> *vitality, because they are in spirit fierce and free,*
> *therefore they want things repeated and unchanged.*
> *They always say, "Do it again"; and the grown-up*
> *person does it again until he is nearly dead. For*
> *grown-up people are not strong enough to exult*
> *in monotony. But perhaps God is strong enough*
> *to exult in monotony. It is possible that God says*
> *every morning, "Do it again" to the sun; and every*
> *evening, "Do it again" to the moon. It may not be*
> *automatic necessity that makes all daisies alike;*
> *it may be that God makes every daisy separately,*
> *but has never got tired of making them. It may be*
> *that he has the eternal appetite of infancy;* ***for we***
> ***have sinned and grown old, and our Father is***
> ***younger than we.***[3]

May we all engage more joyfully in the redemptive human creativity that is our privilege and call—namely, *the hopeful movement toward restoration and renewal.* May we, through an excess of life and vitality, join God in the joyous daily creative work of making space for life and of the reconciliation of all things.

"ALL YOU NEED IS FAITH, TRUST AND A LITTLE PIXIE DUST."

~J.M. BARRIE~
(PETER PAN)

Acknowledgments

More than anyone, I owe a debt of gratitude to my beautiful wife, Tamara. Nobody has poured more time into reviewing and editing the manuscript than she has. Additionally, nobody carries a greater burden while I am in my "writing mode," which she does with the utmost of grace and lovingkindness.

I would like to thank Ben Larson and Tyler Lacoma for their significant partnership and writing help from the inception of this project. Teams make everything better, and that is certainly true in this case.

Emily Hill contributed numerous edits as well as substantial help with research and chasing down citations.

Melissa McCreery, David Jacobsen, Melissa Wuske, and Ed Underwood all graciously provided helpful and insightful editorial reads.

Thank you to Don Jacobson for demonstrating as well as anyone the value of friendship through time and the beauty of godly wisdom.

Thank you also to the team at Moody Publishers for recognizing and valuing what is at the heart of this project. I'd like to especially thank Randall Payleitner for his leadership, Matt Boffey for the invaluable editorial help and creativity, and Erik Peterson for going above and beyond with artistic design.

I am also incredibly grateful to the very talented Paul Crouse who lent considerable time and energy toward illustrating the manuscript and creating custom artwork to make the book more visual, interesting, and powerful.

This book is about the necessity of creativity for us to fully realize who God made us to be. I want to thank the people at Kilns College and Antioch Church in Bend for their continued grace in allowing me to be creative, make mistakes, and dream all over again. You *are* my creative community.

Notes

Chapter 1

1. Madeleine L'Engle, *Walking on Water: Reflections on Faith and Art* (New York: North Point Press, 1980), 89.

2. Robert Epstein, as quoted by Amy Novotney in "The Science of Creativity," *gradPSYCH Magazine*, January 2009, 14.

3. This quote is the widely attributed anecdotal version. However, the original quote is, "Almost everything is imitation. The idea of The Persian Letters was taken from The Turkish Spy. Boiardo imitated Pulci, Ariosto imitated Boiardo. The most original writers borrowed from one another" and appeared in Voltaire's 1733 *Lettres Philosophiques*.

4. *Ex nihilo*, the Latin phrase meaning "out of nothing," is how theologians have long termed this aspect of the doctrine of creation. It means that God didn't create *from* preexisting material, but created the world *from nothing*. He spoke, and the world was.

Chapter 2

1. Online Etymology Dictionary, s.v. "innovation," accessed May 27, 2015, http://etymonline.com/.

2. Nicole Baker Fulgham, email message to author, September 24, 2015.

3. Ron Carter, *Language and Creativity: The Art of Common Talk* (London: Routledge, 2004), 13.

Chapter 3

1. W. J. de Kock, *Out of My Mind: Following the Trajectory of God* (Eugene, OR: Wipf & Stock, 2014), 96. According to Wynand, the Trinity "extended itself and made space for us to grow. It seems quite logical, then, to argue that the love that flows through this relationship to us should also flow through us to others."

2. C. Christopher Smith, email message to author, July 5, 2015.

3. Bruce Schoenfeld, "Why Bend, Ore., Is the Next Big City for Entrepreneurship," *Entrepreneur Magazine,* August 24, 2012.

Chapter 4

1. Judy Martin, "Employee Brain on Stress Can Quash Creativity and Competitive Edge," *Forbes,* September 5, 2012, accessed July 15, 2015, http://www.forbes.com/sites/work-in-progress/2012/09/05/employee-brain-on-stress-can-quash-creativity-competitive-edge/.

Chapter 5

1. Copernicus, as quoted by Dava Sobel in *Galileo's Daughter: A Historical Memoir of Science, Faith, and Love* (New York: Bloomsbury, 1999), 50–51.

2. C. S. Lewis, "On Three Ways of Writing for Children," in *Of Other Worlds: Essays and Stories* (San Fransisco: First Harvest, 1975), 23.

3. C. S. Lewis, dedication in *The Lion, The Witch and The Wardrobe* (New York: HarperCollins, 1950).

4. G. K. Chesterton, *Orthodoxy* (Orlando: Relevant Media Group, 2006), 35.

5. Ibid., 32.

6. Sir Ken Robinson, "Changing Education Paradigms," YouTube, uploaded October 14, 2010, accessed July 14, 2015, https://www.youtube.com/watch?v=zDZFcDGpL4U.

7. George Land and Beth Jarman, *Breakpoint and Beyond: Mastering the Future—Today* (New York: Harper Business, 1992), 153.

8. Sir Ken Robinson, "Changing Education Paradigms."

Chapter 6

1. George Sylvester Viereck, "What Life Means to Einstein," *The Saturday Evening Post*, October 26, 1929, accessed June 26, 2015, http://www.saturdayeveningpost.com/wp-content/uploads/satevepost/what_life_means_to_einstein.pdf.

2. This quotation, widely attributed to a variety of authors, likely stems from Sir Arthur Quiller-Couch's essay "On Style" in *On the Art of Writing* (1916).

3. Steve Jobs, as quoted by Carmine Gallo in "Steve Jobs: Get Rid of the Crappy Stuff," *Forbes*, accessed July 31, 2015, http://www.forbes.com/ sites/carminegallo/2011/05/16/steve-jobs-get-rid-of-the-crappy-stuff/.

4. Daniel Pink, "Think Tank: Flip-thinking—the New Buzzword Sweeping the US," *The Telegraph*, September 10, 2010, accessed July 31, 2015, http://www.telegraph.co.uk/finance/businessclub/7996379/Daniel-Pinks-Think-Tank-Flip-thinking-the-new-buzz-word-sweeping-the-US. html.

Chapter 7

1. Robert Epstein, as quoted by Amy Novotney in "The Science of Creativity," *gradPSYCH Magazine*, January 2009, 14.

2. Stacey Anderson, "When Keith Richards Wrote '(I Can't Get No) Satisfaction' in His Sleep," *Rolling Stone,* May 9, 2011, accessed July 20, 2015, http://www.rollingstone.com/music/news/when-keith-richards-wrote-i-cant-get-no-satisfaction-in-his-sleep-20110509.

3. Jonathan Plucker, as quoted by Amy Novotney in "The Science of Creativity," *gradPSYCH Magazine*, January 2009, 14.

4. Maya Angelou, as quoted by Jeffrey M. Elliot, ed., in *Conversations with Maya Angelou* (Jackson, MI: University Press of Mississippi, 1989), x.

Chapter 8

1. Shane Claiborne, *Red Letter Revolution: What If Jesus Really Meant What He Said?* (Nashville, TN: Thomas Nelson Publishers, 2012), 58.

2. Sir Ken Robinson, "Do Schools Kill Creativity?" YouTube, January 6, 2007, accessed July 14, 2015, https://www.youtube.com/watch?v= iG9CE55wbtY.

3. "Hall of the Prisoners," Accademia.org, accessed April 30, 2015, http:// www.accademia.org/explore-museum/halls/hall-prisoners/.

4. G. K. Chesterton, "The Everlasting Man," in *The Collected Works of G.K. Chesterton* (San Francisco: Ignatius Press, 1986), 388.

5. "Finding Beauty in the Rubble," *Vimeo* video, 4:14, from producers Paul W. Nethercott and Parker Broaddus, posted by "Paul W. Nethercott, Producer," April 15, 2015, accessed July 14, 2015, https://vimeo. com/125076439.

Conclusion

1. John Lennon, "Imagine," in *Imagine,* Apple Records, September 9, 1971.

2. Elizabeth Barrett Browning, *The Complete Works of Mrs. E.B. Browning, vol. 5,* eds. Helen Archibald Clark and Charlotte Endymion Porter (New York: Riverdale Press, 1903), 110.

3. G. K. Chesterton, *Orthodoxy* (Orlando: Relevant Media Group, 2006), 65–66.

About the Author

Ken Wytsma is a leader, innovator, and social entrepreneur. His work takes him around the world as a frequent international speaker on justice and leadership. He's the founder of The Justice Conference, an annual international conference that introduces people to a wide range of organizations and conversations related to biblical justice. He is widely regarded as a thought leader on the topics of justice, human rights, and nonprofit leadership.

In addition to serving as the founding pastor of Antioch Church, Ken is president of Kilns College, where he teaches philosophy, justice, and creative leadership. Ken also served for several years as the executive director of a creative office for World Relief and has experience as a senior partner for a brand strategy and marketing firm.

Ken is the author of *Pursuing Justice* and *The Grand Paradox*. At his blog, kenwytsma.com, he and other experts explore issues of practical theology, creativity, and culture, and the latest ideas related to social enterprise. Ken lives in Bend, Oregon, with his wife, Tamara, and their four daughters.

To contact Ken about speaking at your event, school, or church, or to inquire about creative consulting for your organization, visit kenwytsma.com

NEW MASTER OF ARTS IN
INNOVATION & LEADERSHIP
ONE-YEAR PROGRAM AT KILNS COLLEGE

LEARN *to* CHANGE *the* WORLD

APPLY NOW!
KILNSCOLLEGE.ORG

Online Option Available

ALSO OFFERED:
MASTER OF ARTS IN
BIBLICAL & SOCIAL
JUSTICE

KILNS COLLEGE
GRADUATE SCHOOL OF THEOLOGY & MISSION